D0265780

Donal Harrington

Parish Renewal

VOLUME I

Reflecting on the experience

First edition, 1997, published by
the columba press
55A Spruce Avenue, Stillorgan Industrial Park,
Blackrock, Co Dublin

ISBN 1 85607 186 3

Cover by Bill Bolger
Acorn symbol by Don Conroy
Illustrations by Mark Maguire
Origination by The Columba Press
Printed in Ireland by Colour Books Ltd, Dublin

This book is dedicated to
Dermot O'Mahony and Desmond Williams
who, as auxiliary bishops,
played an inestimable part in initiating and establishing
the parish development and renewal process
in the Dublin diocese.

Contents

Acknowledgements

More than anything else, I want to acknowledge the contribution made to this book by the people involved in parish renewal throughout the diocese, for it is their wisdom that is gathered here. In thanking them, I would mention especially the five area teams and the diocesan committee for parish development and renewal, at present chaired by Bishop Jim Moriarty.

I also acknowledge the contribution made by the priests of the diocese. Time spent with them, both in their parishes and on deanery courses, has greatly deepened my own appreciation of parish renewal.

I acknowledge the generous help of friends and colleagues who read the manuscript. In particular, I thank the other coordinators of the parish renewal process in Dublin – Micheal Comer, Brid Liston, Eilis O'Malley, Tim Hurley, Oonagh O'Brien, Judith King and Julie Kavanagh. In thanking the coordinators, I pay testimony also to the central role played by all the coordinators, past and present, in the progress of renewal in the diocese.

I am very grateful to Mark Maguire for the drawings in the book and for his willingness, as ever, to give his time.

To Paddy Wallace a special word of thanks. As chairman of the coordinators, Paddy's role in shaping and forwarding the renewal process in Dublin was immense. I am very grateful for the many contributions he made to the structure and content of this book.

Thanks to Carol McKiernan in the parish renewal office for all her help. Thanks finally to Seán O Boyle of Columba for his enthusiasm and support.

Foreword

The publication of the two volumes of *Parish Renewal* is indeed a happy event for the Dublin diocese and an occasion for giving thanks to the Lord for the providence that has been experienced through the parish development and renewal process.

Since I became Archbishop I have seen the parish renewal process, which began in the mid-1980s, going from strength to strength. Without prejudice to the acknowledgement of other fine work already going on, the embracing of parish development and renewal in so many of the parishes of the diocese has given great hope. The progress made in such a short time assures us that, despite the obvious difficulties and challenges, the times we are in are heralding a new dawn in the life of the Church.

In this connection I would mention also the diocesan process of preparation for the Jubilee of the year 2000. At my request, the diocesan committee for parish development and renewal has been resourcing this preparation, and already many more parishes are experiencing a new lease of life.

The new dawn regards what has been called the hour of the laity. Parish renewal, as the diocese has come to know it over the last decade, is essentially about men and women sharing in a new way in the responsibility for the future of their parishes. The extent to which this has happened in such a short period of time is testimony to the great faith and commitment among God's people.

This involvement is vividly reflected in the pages of these two volumes. For these volumes represent the experience and wisdom of the many people who have contributed to the advance of renewal in their parishes. In a very real way these people *are* the book.

I take this opportunity to acknowledge the contribution they have made and the new hope they have brought to the life of the Church. I pray with great confidence that this contribution, as it continues into the new Millennium, will bear fruit in plenty for generations to come.

✠ *Desmond Connell*
Archbishop of Dublin

Introduction

In the mid-1980s a process of parish renewal was initiated in the Dublin diocese. In the years since then, the process has expanded and become consolidated in such a way as to make it far and away the most significant pastoral initiative in the diocese in the thirty years since Vatican II.

The intention of this book is to gather together and present the wisdom gained from that experience. The book is in two volumes. The present volume outlines how parish renewal has come to be understood through the experience of the past decade. Volume two is a collection of the resource material – mini-programmes, outlines for meetings and assemblies, evaluation instruments – that have been developed in response to the needs in the parishes.

What Kind of Book?

This first volume is not a 'theological' book in the sense of simply giving the theory or ideal of what the parish is meant to be and to be doing. Nor is it a 'practical' book in the sense of just giving information about initiatives and programmes that work, or of instructing readers in how to carry out such programmes themselves.

Rather, volume one is a theological reflection that emerges out of a process of parish renewal which now involves more than half of the two hundred parishes in the diocese. The process has meant a new experience of Church for many people, a new vitality in many parishes and parish teams, and a new focus and sense of purpose for the diocese. While renewal is a long-term affair and it is still early days, there is little doubt in the diocese that something enduring and of the most profound significance has been initiated.

As a theological reflection, the book presents the way the

process has worked out in Dublin. But perhaps 'theological reflection' is too grand a term. So let us say that the book presents the accumulated wisdom of the last ten years. In part this wisdom is a knowledge of how to go about parish renewal. Perhaps more importantly, it is what has been learned about the nature of parish renewal as such, its context and foundations and principles and dynamics. Without this kind of wisdom the 'how to go about it' would be very superficial.

The book is not telling the reader 'this is how you should do it'. Rather, it is saying 'this is what we have come to know' (it is 'theology' in that sense). It has the authority of experience – the experience of a very large number of parishes, of parishioners, of priests.

Some of it could have been written ten years ago. But the heart of it could not have been expressed that long ago, for so much of what the book contains has been *learned through the experience of renewal*. This I take to be the spirit of 'praxis' – not the application of theory to practice, but practising on the basis of an inchoate vision, only for the experience of the practice to generate a wisdom – a 'theory' – that would not otherwise have come into being.

In this sense also, the book is not the idea of any one person, even if it is one author's synthesis. It represents the collective wisdom of those who have been involved in the process throughout the diocese and hopefully it does so faithfully.

The Structure of this Volume

The sequence of chapters is intended to be cumulative. An *introductory chapter* gives an overview of the Dublin experience and presents the main insights learned from that experience – these will be elaborated on in parts one and two. Part one of the volume concerns the overall picture. Part two goes into the dynamics.

The chapters of *part one* tease out the meaning of the new mindset of 'mission' that underlies the whole process. Chapter two considers the challenge to hope as fundamental in renewal. Chapter three explores the distinction between 'spirituality' and 'religion' as one which provides the basis, in the following chapters, for articulating a new understanding of parish. Chapter four offers a vision of parish. Chapter five goes into what is meant by speaking of the parish of the future as *missionary*.

Chapter six teases out what the mission of the parish is trying to achieve.

The chapters of *part two* focus on the 'how' of the parish of the future, that 'how' being the way of shared responsibility or collaboration. In chapter seven, the theme of collaboration is located at the heart of the Christian gospel. Chapters eight and nine look at collaboration in relation to what it means to be a parishioner. Chapter ten looks at collaboration in relation to what it means to be a priest.

Chapter eleven studies the dynamics of collaboration in practice between priests and parishioners, identifying the key elements whereby the process is made or broken. Chapter twelve does the same for meetings; it is included because meetings are where 'the rubber meets the road', where it is evident whether collaboration is real or merely notional. Chapter thirteen is a concluding reflection.

At the end of each of the chapters of parts one and two, there are cross-references to the corresponding resource materials in volume two. These materials are the mini-programmes that have been developed in response to what has been coming up in the parishes. In the references at the end of each chapter, it is indicated exactly where the main ideas and issues of that chapter are treated in volume two.

This brings us back again to the interplay of theory and practice. On the one hand, there is the 'theology' of parish renewal. On the other, there is the 'practice' of parish renewal. I hope that the cross-referencing between volumes one and two communicates how intimately the theology and the practice are interwoven. The theology presented in volume one is nothing other than the wisdom of the parishes. The practice reflected in the resource material of volume two is itself the articulation of a theology.

Providence

One document referred to repeatedly is Pope John Paul II's encyclical letter, *Christifideles Laici,* on the vocation and mission of the laity, which arose out of the Synod on the Laity that had just taken place. The document came out just as the Dublin process was getting off the ground. In this a providence was seen, a providence identified by Archbishop Desmond Connell in his discerning that *Christifideles Laici* gave the process of renewal in Dublin the focus it needed.

A further providence has been seen in the Pope's more recent apostolic letter, *Tertio Millennio Adveniente* on the forthcoming jubilee of the year 2000. This letter has given a new impetus to the process of renewal, inviting the people of the parishes, at this special time, to assume responsibility for their own future as God's people.

Providence is at the heart of parish renewal. Very many people have put their hearts into the work. Very many have been spiritually transformed by the experience. In all of this, there is a lively sense that God's Spirit is at work. In the words of St Paul (Philippians 1: 6), there is a confidence that God, who began this good work, will see it brought to completion.

Note: I usually refer to *Christifideles Laici* as 'CFL'. Another document quoted a number of times, *The Sign We Give*, by the Bishops' Conference of England and Wales, is referred to simply as *The Sign We Give.*

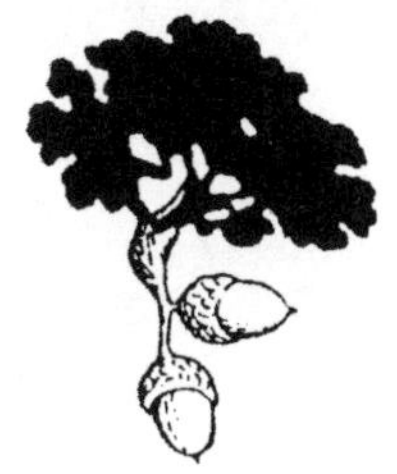

CHAPTER 1

Overview: The experience of parish renewal

This volume is a gathering together of what has been learned about parish renewal from the experience of the Dublin diocese over the past ten years. But before being presented with what has been learned, it may help the reader to have some overall familiarity with the experience itself. To this end I will first give some information about how the process has evolved in the diocese and in the parishes. Then I will briefly present five key insights that have been learned from the process. The remaining chapters can be seen as elaborating on these insights.

What is presented here is not offered as a blueprint, for every diocese can and should go its own way. It is offered as something which has been working very well and which contains insights that would be relevant to any parish. In this regard I would note the *variety* of parishes in which the process has been evolving, ranging from suburban to rural to inner city, and from more affluent to more deprived contexts.

THE DUBLIN EXPERIENCE

In 1985, the then archbishop, Kevin McNamara, set up a diocesan committee for 'parish development and renewal' (referred to simply as parish renewal in what follows). The committee included two of the auxiliary bishops, together with priests, laity and religious. Its brief was to research and to facilitate a process of renewal in the parishes.

Priorities

In this spirit, the committee began with a process of consultation. While there was a certain amount of consultation with parishes, the main consultation, as it happened, was with the priests of the diocese. Two questions were asked:

(1) What needs should be addressed in any parish renewal process?

(2) What help would you look for from the diocese?

From the response to the first question, four priorities regarding renewal emerged. They were (in order of priority): lay participation, adult faith formation, renewal of priests and youth ministry. A follow-up consultation sharpened the findings. Not alone was lay participation confirmed as the first priority, but it was seen as fundamental to all else.

The responses to the second question identified the need for a pastoral resource centre, for pastoral expertise to assist the parishes, for consultation and for a pastoral policy in the diocese. But the main thrust of the responses was that the most important help to parishes would be, not resource materials or a resource centre, but resource persons who would work with the parishes in responding to the demands of renewal.

I think it is worth emphasising how this consultation contains in embryo so much of what was to follow. Beginning with consultation was a statement that nothing was to be imposed on the diocese. Indeed, some 'pre-packaged' renewal programmes from other countries had been rejected on these very grounds. The process was to be one of listening and of responding to what emerged. The agenda would be set, not from outside, but by priests and parishioners, in a spirit of listening, entering into a shared responsibility for the future of their parishes.

Personnel

Following the consultations, the committee made its report and gave its recommendations to the archbishop. By the summer of 1988 six full-time personnel had been appointed as pastoral renewal coordinators in the diocese, one in each of the five auxiliary bishops'areas (each comprising about forty parishes) and one overall coordinator. The role of these coordinators was to be one of helping initiate a process of renewal in the parishes and of facilitating, supporting and resourcing the process.

In addition, each bishop formed an 'area team' which included people from the area, both priests and religious and parishioners, as well as the bishop himself and the local and overall coordinators of parish renewal. Meanwhile the overall diocesan committee continued to function, now in a new role of overseeing the process in the diocese as a whole and mapping future directions in the light of the evolving process.

The area teams are dedicated to reflecting on the progress of parish renewal in their areas, to discerning needs and possible developments, and to elaborating ways of encouraging that development. One of the main initiatives of the area teams has been their bringing together the parishes in their areas on various occasions. The sharing of experience that this has enabled has been an enormous source of encouragement to the parish groups.

No less significant is the way in which the area teams themselves demonstrate the spirit of collaboration, between bishops and priests and religious and parishioners. In this they are committed to realising in their own operating that spirit which they seek to engender in the parishes.

The area coordinators have included both married and single, male and female, priests and religious. As they began their work, the need for further help in resourcing the process in the parishes became evident. To this end a part-time coordinator was appointed in 1991, with responsibility for developing resources and for exploring ways of linking the various diocesan agencies and personnel into the parish renewal process. In 1996 a further full-time person was appointed to work in this area.

Even though progress is gradual, the fact is that since the appointment of the full-time coordinators in 1988, more than half of the two hundred parishes in the dioceses have, of their own volition, become involved. In a very short time, therefore, the process of parish renewal by way of shared responsibility between priests and parishioners has become the pattern in the diocese. Its acceptance by so many parishes and its confirmation by the archbishop constitute it as a source of great hope for the decades ahead.

The End is in the Means

To my mind, what comes across most strikingly from this brief history is the importance of the *how* over the *what*. At every stage, success has been the fruit of things being done in a certain way, namely in the spirit of listening and collaboration. This is true both of the initial consultations in the diocese, of the initiation of the process in individual parishes, and of the work of the area teams and the diocesan committee.

Obversely, the common pattern where things have not gone well is not about what was done, but about the way in which things were done. When parish renewal runs into difficulty it is because of the challenge of the *process* rather than the challenge of the task. The difficulties are difficulties that priests and parishioners have with collaborating and sharing responsibility. The ends of parish renewal are *in* the means. The *how* is all important.

TWO TYPICAL PATTERNS

The experience of renewal has been different in each parish; there is no one path for everybody to follow. But it has not been totally different. Amidst the diversity of what happens, it has been possible to identify common patterns across parishes. In Dublin two such typical patterns have been identified from the experience so far in over a hundred parishes.

One pattern is to start from a small base, the other is to establish a broad base first. Both, however, begin in the same way, namely, with the priests of the parish. Because parish renewal is never imposed, it only begins at the invitation of the parish personnel. Therefore the first step always is to meet the parish priest, or all the priests together, or the parish team if religious and/or parishioners are already involved at this level (see volume two, *The Priest and Parish Renewal*).

This meeting with the parish team could extend over a number of sessions. Indeed, this stage is so crucial to the whole process that it is worth a lot of time. It is quite possible that the priests have never worked together themselves up to this. There may be quite a lot of work to be done in bonding them together, in encouraging mutual affirmation in their different styles of ministry, and in facilitating the emergence of a common vision and hope for the parish.

Then there is the work of explaining what parish renewal is about, of ensuring everybody's understanding and acceptance of the key ideas, particularly the idea of collaboration, and of deciding the best way to begin. It is at this stage that parishes head off along slightly different paths.

Beginning Small

On the one hand there are those who begin on a small scale.

What usually happens is that the priests or parish team gather a small number of parishioners (fifteen to thirty) to engage with them in the *Called by Name* course (see volume two). These parishioners might be representative of different groups in the parish or they might be invited simply in their own right. While there will be an open invitation to all in the parish to participate, experience suggests strongly that personal contact is vital.

Called by Name is a set of six sessions on the foundational themes of vocation, communion and mission, designed to bring the group to a common vision and shared understanding concerning parish renewal. By the end of the course, a smaller group, perhaps twelve to fifteen people, are willing to continue. This group of priests and parishioners form a 'core group', sharing responsibility for the overall care of the process of renewal in the parish.

The next step is for the group to identify the needs of the parish. This is where the process broadens out to give voice to the parish as a whole. The most common way of going about this is by way of a parish assembly (see volume two, *Parish Assemblies*). These assemblies begin by acknowledging the signs of hope present in the parish, and then go on to identify and prioritise the needs of the parish.

Working groups can then be set up to address the different needs. These groups begin by undertaking whatever formation or training is desirable in order to equip them for their work. The areas of need that tend to come up in parish after parish are liturgy, adult religious education, care for people in need, ministry to youth, prayer, and communications in the parish.

Meanwhile the core group has to attend to its own development. A decision has to be made as to what kind of operating structure it will adopt (see volume two, *Choosing a Model of Operating*). This is a decision as to (a) what level of collaboration and shared decision-making there will be between priests and parishioners, and (b) what kind of relationship there will be between the core group and other groups in the parish.

As well as attending to its own needs, the core group must consider ways of expanding the process in the parish, so as to make the experience of *participation* as real as possible for as many as possible. At this point, the group also needs to address the need for ongoing *evaluation* of the whole process.

PARISH RENEWAL – TWO TYPICAL PATHS

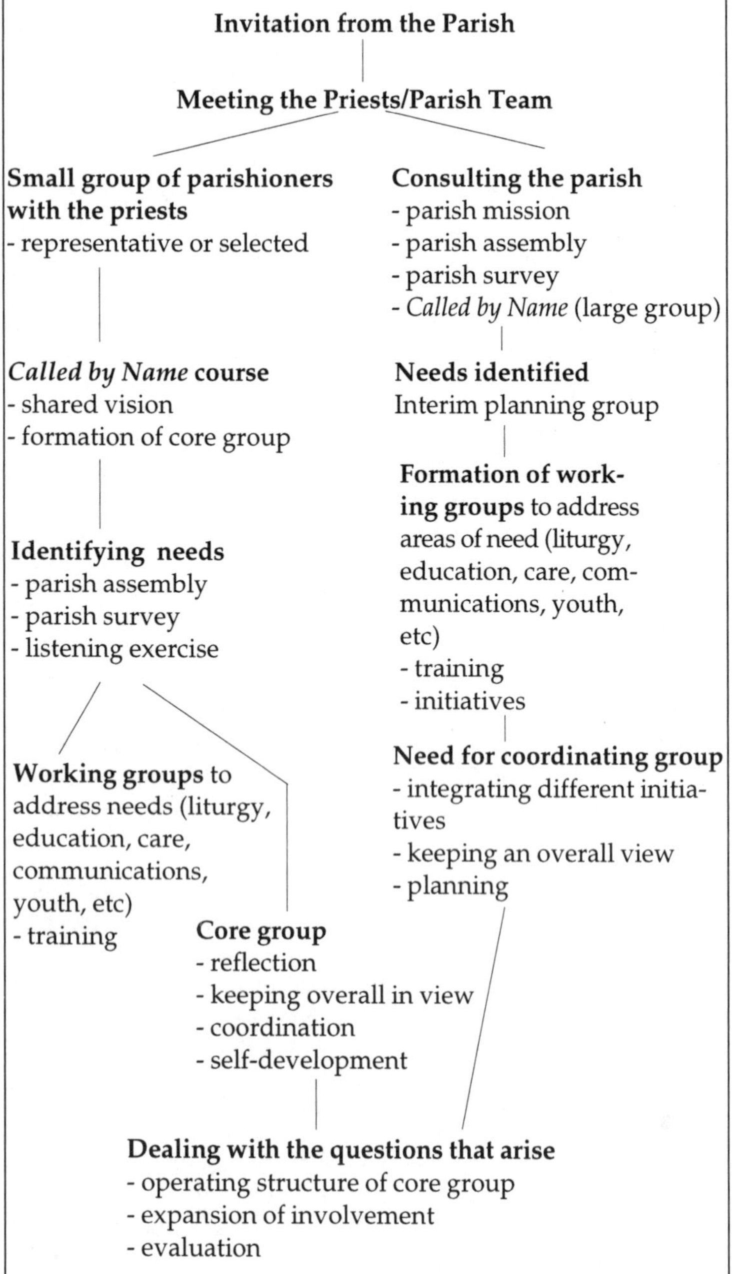

Invitation from the Parish

Meeting the Priests/Parish Team

Small group of parishioners with the priests
- representative or selected

***Called by Name* course**
- shared vision
- formation of core group

Identifying needs
- parish assembly
- parish survey
- listening exercise

Working groups to address needs (liturgy, education, care, communications, youth, etc)
- training

Core group
- reflection
- keeping overall in view
- coordination
- self-development

Consulting the parish
- parish mission
- parish assembly
- parish survey
- *Called by Name* (large group)

Needs identified
Interim planning group

Formation of working groups to address areas of need (liturgy, education, care, communications, youth, etc)
- training
- initiatives

Need for coordinating group
- integrating different initiatives
- keeping an overall view
- planning

Dealing with the questions that arise
- operating structure of core group
- expansion of involvement
- evaluation

Beginning Broad

On the other hand there are parishes which begin on a broad scale. Here the priests or parish team opt to bring in the entire parish from the beginning, usually through a parish assembly. Some parishes plan a parish mission as a way of initiating renewal in the parish, followed by an assembly. Others have put on the *Called by Name* course for a large number of people as a way of starting on a broad scale.

Whichever of these is chosen, the outcome is that a large number of parishioners have been involved and consulted at a very early stage. Once the needs of the parish have been identified, people can volunteer for the different working groups. After appropriate training, these groups can get down to planning initiatives.

Meanwhile, the need will be felt for some form of overall coordinating group. This can develop subsequently into a more permanent core group, keeping the overall picture in view, integrating the different initiatives and planning ahead. As above, such a group will also have to attend to its own operating structure, to its link with other parish groups, to the question of expansion, and to the evaluation of the process.

These are the two typical patterns. No one parish will be exactly like what I have outlined, but all will be able to identify more or less with either. But the two are not that dissimilar. In both there is some form of collaborative group taking overall responsibility for the process of renewal in the parish. In both the whole parish is consulted, be it sooner or later. And in both, what is to be done emerges out of a process of listening.

The Dublin diocese comprises a wide variety of parishes, from inner city to affluent suburban to depressed suburban to rural. These contexts are quite different in many respects, such as community morale, availability locally of resources and resource persons, the profile of the church.

Nevertheless, the typical patterns still stand. This is because the focus is not on providing programmes devised in the abstract, but on helping people think through their own situation. The experience has been that the process thus initiated tends to run along either of these two lines.

MISSION: THE NEW MINDSET

I now wish to turn to what has been learned about parish renewal from the experience of the past ten years. Learning from experience is a hallmark of parish renewal and there are *five insights* or learnings that stand out in the Dublin experience. That is not to say that these insights are unique to Dublin, but simply that they stand out as the distinctive aspects of parish renewal as it has come to be understood.

The *first insight* is that parish renewal is grounded in the mindset of 'mission'. The phrase 'a new mindset' is one that was used by Pope Paul VI when introducing the new Code of Canon Law in the early 1970s. The phrase – in Latin, *novus habitus mentis* – obviously refers to the spirit of Vatican II. But there is also a sense in which the phrase is 'left there' for its meaning to be discovered by those who enter into exploring it. This is not the same as saying that it can mean whatever people want it to mean. It is saying that the phrase expresses an intuition into truth and that the intuition awaits elaboration.

One way of elaborating is by reflecting on the phenomenon of change. Change has figured large in our experience of Church for some decades now. But change is not simply something that happens to the Church. It is also something that happens in ourselves. Thus one parish priest spoke of coming to the realisation that 'the only person I can change is myself'. This is in fact a cornerstone of parish renewal – the change that happens in individuals who become involved in the process, a change upon which the viability of the process critically depends.

The 'new mindset' refers to this change and we reflect on it in part one of this volume. There, it is presented as revolving around the theme of 'mission'. Parish renewal, as it has come to be understood in Dublin, demands of each of us that we think of the parish in terms of mission. The word 'mission', of course, is not foreign to the parish – after all, we have parish missions and we pray in our churches for the missions. But it is 'foreign' in the other sense that missionary work has been understood to refer *only* to work done in foreign lands.

To think of *our* parish *primarily* in terms of mission is to think of it in a very different way than heretofore. The change required in our mindset is quite significant and not to be underestimated.

It makes for a new mode of being-in the parish and for a refocusing of time and energy. While the transformation is not easily achieved, it is absolutely essential to the success of renewal.

THE 'MINISTERING PARISH'

The *second insight* concerns the aim of parish renewal and the criterion of its success. This is what is expressed in the concept of what has been called 'the ministering parish'. Again, the idea is not unique to Dublin but it has come to a particularly sharp focus as the process has evolved in the diocese.

The Parish of Ministries

Experience reveals that many priests and parish workers are satisfied with what has been called a 'parish of ministries'. For them, this would constitute a successful parish. It is what many others, in parishes with a low level of activity, aspire to. In a parish of ministries, parish life is very well organised, there are lots of activities catering for many different people and many different needs, and there are many 'ministers' involved in providing these services, be they church-based or community-based.

But experience has also shown up a certain dissatisfaction with the parish of ministries. Not that it is not very good in itself to have so much going on and so well organised, especially considering that many parishes do not even have this much. Yet, while everything appears to be running so smoothly, there is an underlying feeling that something is missing, even that everything is too 'sewn-up'.

Partly it has something to do with the '100%' who make up the parish. It is a sense that even a successful parish of ministries leaves many of God's people untouched. It is a sense that too much activity is church-centred (i.e. the parish buildings), therefore failing to reach many who do not come into contact with the 'visible' parish.

It is also a sense of fragmentation. There may be many things going on, but without that much communication or coordination between the different activities. Everything is in its own little box and there is often felt to be a lack of overall purpose and direction. The music at Mass is uplifting, the ministers bring communion to the sick, the parish finance committee works wonders, and so on; but what is the vision that inspires?

Not unrelated to this, the parish of ministries is in fact compatible with a continuing hierarchialism in the parish. Lots may be happening, but the priest may still be very much in control and calling the shots. There may be little sense of 'ownership' of the process by others. There may be effectively no collaboration at all. What seems at first sight to be a 'people's church' turns out to be something quite different. Sometimes, when the priest moves on and is replaced by another, it becomes clear how much hinged on him and him alone.

The Ministering Parish

These kinds of reactions have led to a richer and deeper formulation of the goal of parish renewal in terms of the ministry of *all* God's people in the parish (chapters eight and nine elaborate on this). What this means is that the successful parish is one where all God's people are entering more and more into the adventure of being disciples of Christ in their ordinary, everyday lives.

This does not mean that everybody has to be involved in some parish group or some official ministry in the parish. It means that all God's people in the parish would have the sense of welcome and belonging. It means that all would feel encouraged to live their Christian faith in the circumstances of their daily lives. It means that their coming to church would nourish their life of discipleship. All 'ministries' and all collaborative leadership are at the service of this.

In a way, this seems obvious enough. As against that, we have to look at how many parishes think of success in terms of a parish of ministries. We also have to look at how many books about ministry say that all God's people are called to ministry, and then go on to describe ministry in terms of public, official-type parish ministries that the vast majority of God's people will never be involved in.

In other words, the centrality of the 'ministering parish' represents an insight into what being 'involved' in the parish or 'participating' in the parish is about. Being involved does not mean doing things. It is about the integration of faith and life. It is about a sense of belonging.

THE WAY OF COLLABORATION

The *third insight* of the new mindset is about the way in which the parish goes about its mission of reaching out to all God's people. This is what is referred to by terms such as 'partnership', 'shared responsibility', 'collaboration 'and 'participation' The new mindset is expressed in this new way of doing things and of being together in the parish.

In the Dublin experience, it has come to be seen that parish renewal hinges on parishioners and priests learning to be together in a new way (this is explored in chapters nine and ten). Here again, new habits of mind are demanded of both. In the parish as it has been, priests and parishioners were 'with' each other in a different way. It was a way where priests carried the responsibility for the parish on their own. Without commenting on how well or badly this worked for its own time, its time has passed.

The new way of collaboration or shared responsibility is what today's wisdom points to as the way forward for the parish. Sharing responsibility for the future of the parish means that parishioners and priests will be together differently than previously. As one parishioner put it, priests have to talk to parishioners in a new way; parishioners have to talk to priests in a new way; priests have to talk to priests in a new way; and parishioners have to talk to parishioners in a new way.

In the new mindset, priests and parishioners talk together about the most important things in the parish. This does not come easily; it is a *novus habitus mentis,* a new habit of mind, and a change from what was previously habitual takes time. It is an unravelling and a reweaving of our mutual consciousness as priests and parishioners. This is what part two of this volume explores.

Successes and Failures

This is an appropriate point at which to say something about the difference that renewal makes in parishes. It is appropriate because the most important differences, the key successes and failures, have to do with the issue of collaboration.

While most parishes in the Dublin diocese have some commitment to renewal, progress is slow. Addressing the big challenges such as outreach to the inactive or ministry to youth is still in its early days – the process is, after all, a long-term one. Most of the effort up to now has, understandably, gone into facilitating change in those who are already committed, both parishioners and priests.

Here, the difference has been profound. Where the process has got off the ground, both priests and parishioners talk of how the experience of collaboration has changed them. Parishioners speak of having found a voice, of having discovered the confidence to take initiatives and assume leadership, of feeling a responsibility for the mission of the Church. Priests speak of the affirmation and new energy the process has meant for them. They speak of a transformation in their experience of priesthood.

In addition to this, people speak of a new vitality in the parish. There is a sense that something new is happening. This is reflected in a new quality of liturgy, in a new mood of hospitality, in a renewed sense of care, in better communications and in other new initiatives. Most of all, where the spirit of collaboration is real, this spirit spreads out to the parish, in a sense that a 'people's Church' is being born again.

As regards failures, these (as I have already said) have mainly to do with the quality of collaboration. Failure is almost always due to an inability or unwillingness to take on the new mindset. This failure may be on the part either of the priests or the people of the parish (chapters nine and ten explore the reasons for this).

Nevertheless, it deserves to be underlined, frightening though it sounds, that the greatest single cause of failure is the priest who blocks the process. In no case has it happened that the process came to a halt where the priests were committed to collaboration.

AN INDIGENOUS PROCESS

The *fourth insight* is about 'process'. The theme of process pervades the two volumes of this book. It is reflected upon most explicitly in chapters eleven and twelve of volume one and in session five of *The Core Group and Parish Renewal* in volume two. The idea is often hard to grasp and to explain, yet it is a *sine qua non* of parish renewal. When the shift of mindset towards thinking in terms of process is taking place, parish renewal flourishes.

Here I would refer again to that significant moment at the initiation of the current parish renewal movement in Dublin. After some research it was decided not to adopt any of the excellent programmes developed abroad. Instead, consultation in the diocese revealed the priority of lay participation and of providing resource persons to facilitate this participation at all levels of parish life.

So, in other words, instead of proposing any one programme of renewal to the parishes, the diocese offered to help each parish to initiate and sustain its own process of renewal. The only parameters were those already indicated in the consultation, those of lay participation and partnership, where God's people would be actively involved in the mission of the Church in their own place. After that each parish would, with help from without, discern for itself its own way forward.

As the parishes proceeded in this spirit there were, as would be expected, similarities in what emerged. But more significant than such similarities is the indigenous nature of what emerged. Renewal remains indigenous and ongoing in each parish in a way in which, I believe, any pre-packaged programme of renewal that might have been adopted could never be. Each parish owns its own renewal and that renewal has the character of an organic growth.

In the end, parish renewal is not about programmes, but about people. It is not about following a well-worn trail, but about the people of the parish discerning for themselves the way forward. They will adopt various programmes along the way, but as part of their own unique process

This distinction between process and programme may not have been invented in Dublin, but it remains one of the most distinctive aspects of the experience. However, there are quite a number of individuals and groups and agencies engaged in pastoral activity who think predominantly in terms of programmes rather than process. Often it has been the dialogue with these others which has brought home to those engaged in parish renewal the central importance of the mindset of process.

Core Groups and Pastoral Councils

This is an appropriate context for a comment about core groups and pastoral councils. It is notable that parishes involved in the Dublin parish renewal process rarely, if ever, opt to set up a 'parish council' *or* a 'pastoral council'. This contrasts with the path taken by many parishes in other dioceses. The contrast is largely accounted for, I believe, by the emphasis on process.

There are, of course, strong similarities between core groups and pastoral councils. Both are made up of priests and parishioners. Both are of a similar size. Both are intended to express the co-responsibility of all for the life of the parish. Both are exercises in collaboration.

But there is also a difference, and it has to do with the indigenous nature of renewal in the Dublin experience. When renewal by way of shared responsibility is understood as an indigenous process, the agenda is set *in via* by the parish itself. It may well be that typical patterns emerge, for instance, that most parishes will end up forming a core group. But predicting is not presuming; each parish decides for itself how it will proceed.

In contrast to this, when a pastoral council is set up, its eventual format will often have been envisaged from very early on. Often it will have been envisaged in some detail – for instance, that the membership shall be representative of different parish groups, that the parish priest shall be in the chair, that certain structures and procedures shall be adhered to. This emphasis on a predetermined structure is more true of parish councils than of pastoral councils.

Each emphasis, that on structure and that on process, has its strengths and weaknesses. Emphasising structure makes for clarity of purpose, but the group can find its energy absorbed by tasks and administration, and even by power struggles. Emphasising process keeps the group focused on the centrality of vision and of collaboration, but it can also be vague and frustrating.

However, the differences can be exaggerated. Perhaps the resolution is to be found in the insight that process precedes structure. Experience indicates that the priority is to get the process right and to think in terms of people learning to collaborate. Once this is working well, the question of more permanent structures can emerge in its own good time.

THE DIOCESAN DIMENSION

The *fifth insight* concerns the 'outsider' dimension of parish renewal. Parish renewal in Dublin is a *diocesan* activity or project. This means that there is an 'outside the parish' dimension to it, which is not there in the same way when any parish goes alone.

The experience up to now has confirmed the centrality of this dimension in promoting renewal in the parishes.

The Coordinator

First of all, there is the value of the full-time coordinators appointed by the diocese. These appointments are a concrete statement of the resolve of the diocese and its commitment to the process. From the point of view of the parishes these coordinators have proved to be a key factor in initiating and sustaining the process.

Very many parishes would still be 'stuck' were it not for the coordinator. As both 'insider' and 'outsider' the coordinator is a sign of hope for the parish, encouraging people to keep going, drawing on the experience of other parishes, and putting parishes in touch with resources and resource personnel at critical moments.

I was struck to hear recently of one Irish company which employs five people whose sole task is to be *facilitators of change* in the company and its personnel. The description fits the coordinators well. Recalling what I said above about change, the coordinator is the person whose presence has proved pivotal in facilitating the change to a new mindset in parish personnel and in parishioners.

Resource Persons

Secondly, there is the value of the resource persons whom the coordinator links to the parishes. These resource people assist the parishes in responding to the needs as they emerge in and are defined by the parishes themselves. Up to now the resource persons in question have most often been people with catechetical skills in areas such as adult religious education, liturgy and spirituality. But also, resource persons with facilitation and group-work skills have been becoming more and more significant.

As the coordinators and resource personnel have engaged with the parishes, a direct link has become evident between the quality of these persons and the quality of the response within the parishes. The main qualities of resource persons I have in mind here are their competence and professionalism in their fields of expertise, and their capacity to work in harmony with the process and philosophy of parish renewal.

As the 'insider-outsider' dynamic unfolds, with the right resource person facilitating people in the parish towards offering themselves for collaborative ministry, people *have* tended to become involved. It may only be a certain number of people, but it has always been found to be enough.

More and more today, the need is being felt for the appointment of full-time lay people to ministry in the Church. One reaction to the current situation is to bemoan the lack of such appointments. Another reaction is to see the full-time coordinators and the resource persons already working in parishes as a very significant step in the direction of what so many desire.

Resource Materials

Thirdly, when parish renewal is taken on by the diocese as a whole, resources become available that would never have existed if it was a case of individual parishes working away on their own. Volume two of this book details the resource materials developed up to now in the Dublin diocese.

These mini-programmes have been developed, not in a vacuum, but precisely in response to the needs arising in the parishes. Hence they are totally rooted in what is happening in and what is needed by the parishes. They have a quality of 'this is what works'.

An important aspect of these mini-programmes or courses is their flexibility. Because the resource persons are in tune with the process and philosophy of parish renewal, they can adapt the resource materials to the situation of the particular group. This flexibility highlights the centrality of 'process'.

Togetherness

When it is the diocese which takes on the process of renewal, this means that the diocese as a whole is linked in a common mission. Equally, of course it can happen in a diocese that the renewal initiated by individual parishes expands so as to take on the character of a diocesan movement. *Ní neart go cur le chéile* – strength is born of togetherness. This is true enough when an individual parish learns the spirit of collaboration. Its truth is multiplied when a diocese commits itself to the path of renewal.

For one thing it means that the parish is not alone. So many who strive for renewal in the Church seem to be ploughing a lone furrow. Their isolation weighs them down and makes it hard to keep up hope. In stark contrast, there is huge encouragement generated when parishes are striving towards a common goal. The area teams play a central role here through the simple exercise of bringing parish groups together.

The letter to the Hebrews, after recounting the example of faith of Abraham and Moses and so many others after them, continues: 'since we are surrounded by so great a cloud of witnesses, let us also lay aside every weight… and let us run with perseverance the race that is set before us' (Hebrews 12: 1). Likewise in parish renewal, when people in the parish discover they are part of a great throng, the lift this gives is remarkable.

This is all the more important when we consider that success does not come quickly or dramatically. Everybody who goes down the road of collaboration knows how gradual it is and how formidable the obstacles can be. It takes time to learn to work together and to achieve a common focus. It takes a lot of work to reach out to the whole parish. It takes courage to keep going when the response is disappointing. It is hard to bounce back when there is a change in parish personnel and the new arrival is not supportive. It takes patience to persevere when results do not come in quickly.

In such circumstances, it is a great boost to meet other parishes and to discover that they are in the same boat. Somehow a difficulty is not such a difficulty when it is also somebody else's difficulty! It has been the repeated experience in the Dublin diocese that when parish groups engaged in renewal come together for some purpose and share their experience, the energy generated leaves everybody going home with new commitment and a new patience with the gradual nature of the process.

Sharing Wisdom

Besides this simple human support, there is the possibility of sharing wisdom, when other parishes are travelling the same path. Sharing experience can be the occasion of new insight, as parishes learn from the successes and failures of each other. Even if the experiences are dissimilar, the very contrast can be what helps people understand their own situation more clearly. Even when parishes do not actually meet, part of the role of the coordinator is to draw on the experience of other parishes, in order to avoid repetition of the same mistakes and in order to discern better amongst possible ways forward.

None of this is meant to suggest that a parish can get nowhere on its own. Of course it can. It is to suggest, rather, that when we think about parish renewal we would do well to think of it as something the diocese takes on and not just something that individual parishes decide upon. For, when it is taken on by the diocese as a whole, parish renewal is transformed into a different thing entirely.

PART I

Thinking about the parish in a new way

CHAPTER 2

Today's Church: Challenged to hope

In the story of the Church down the centuries there have been many ups and downs, times of tranquillity and times of turbulence. It is a paradox of this history that the Church can be most alive when it is most under threat and that it can grow complacent when everything is going well. No doubt this testifies to a more general truth, that times of crisis can lead us to rediscover what we really are.

The time we live in now is widely regarded as a time of crisis for the Church, but it is also a time of rediscovery. There are so many things that give us cause for anxiety, but amongst them there are also to be found seeds of hope and possibilities for rebirth. The movement of parish renewal that has been gathering momentum in recent years is one of the great signs of hope, inspiring new confidence in God's providence.

FEELINGS

If we were to consult a cross-section of Christians today we would come in contact with a variety of feelings about the situation of the Church. Some are confused, unable to understand the significance of what is happening. They hear some voices telling them that the issue is simply that of restoring the practices that flourished a few decades ago. They hear others telling them that we are now living in a 'post-Christian' era, that religion has had its day. It can be hard to know what to think.

Others feel apprehension, as they look towards the future. They feel that, with the advent of the scientific and technological age, the magic seems to have gone out of religion. Appeals to divine powers and divine authority carry little weight or credibility. The suspicion grows that perhaps God has not been in this at all, and that we are simply seeing the end of a once very powerful human institution.

Others look back in time, with feelings of despondency, disappointment and even betrayal. They fondly recall the Church they grew up in and which has meant so much to them. They are genuinely sad that so much of it has disappeared. They cannot understand why it does not mean the same to so many of the generation that has come after them. Sometimes they blame the world we are living in. Sometimes they feel let down by the Church itself.

Then there are the feelings of those who have been working for change in the Church. The morale of many is quite low and some have given up. Others feel helpless, or are caught in a feeling of inertia. Others are angry at the Church's own failure to adapt to the challenges, and frustrated at the lack of opportunity to channel their commitment.

Finally there are the positive feelings. I remember listening to a parish priest speaking to a group of students a few years ago about priesthood. He proclaimed that this is the most optimistic of times, a great time to be a priest. It reminds me of the lines, 'Two men look out through the same bars; One sees the mud, and one the stars.' Besides the many who are disappointed or confused or apprehensive, there are many others who are filled with a sense of adventure and confidence.

THE GOD OF HOPE

This sense of confidence is what inspires this book, but it is a sense of confidence that also feels the disappointment, confusion and apprehension. Such a seemingly contradictory combination of feelings is in fact what hope is all about.

Christian Hope

There is no doubt that, of Paul's three abiding virtues of faith, hope and love (1 Corinthians 13: 13), hope has been the neglected one. There is no end of Christian literature on love, and much has been written too about faith. But there has been very little on hope. Yet hope is arguably the Christian virtue most needed in these times of adversity for the church.

What Christian hope asserts essentially is the sense of possibility in every situation. The basis for this confidence to be found in a truth which, it seems to me, is absolutely fundamental to being a Christian. This truth is expressed succinctly by St Paul in his letter to the Romans, when he says: 'We know that all things work together for good for those who love God' (Romans 8:28). Sometimes this is translated, 'in everything God works for the good'.

The statement expresses a conviction about God's providence, the assurance that in every situation God's purposes *are* being achieved, God's will *is* being done. When we reflect on it, it is hard to see what being a Christian could mean without something of this conviction.

The justification for such a radical confidence lies in the Easter mystery of the death and resurrection of Jesus. God's presence in the darkness of Gethsemane and Calvary, raising Jesus from death to life, means that the power of the Easter mystery is at work in every situation and every darkness. If God was working for the good in this, the low point of all human history, then we may be sure that God works for the good in everything

This means no less than that the Easter or 'paschal' mystery, the mystery of death transformed to life, is the basic pattern of reality. Christians are called to see all reality from this perspective. In every situation they are asked to believe that God is working for the good, that God's purposes are being achieved. Thus Christianity is essentially the practice of hope.

Amazement

One of the most striking illustrations of what this means comes from the second book of Isaiah (Isaiah 40-55). The book concerns a situation far more grave than our own. The people had lost everything, their temple and their land, as they wept by the waters of Babylon. Yet in that desolation God announces: 'Do not remember the former things, or consider the things of old. I am about to do a new thing; now it springs forth, do you not perceive it? I will make a way in the wilderness and rivers in the desert' (Isaiah 43: 18-19).

Another word for this hope is *amazement*. Hope is our amazement at what God does, again and again bringing life out of death. As we reflect in amazement on how this has happened in the past, we become disposed to being amazed also by what God is doing today.

Another way of putting it would be to say that the Christian

God is a God of newness, 'about to do a new thing' as Isaiah says. And in the very last pages of the Bible we read: 'And the one who was seated on the throne said, 'See, I am making all things new'' (Revelation 21: 5).

To say that reality has a paschal pattern is to say that God is constantly making all things new, forever bringing life out of death. In the words of the psalm, God sends forth God's Spirit, renewing the face of the earth (Psalm 104: 30). The work of parish renewal is a cooperation with this, God's own work of renewal.

There is one important qualification to make here, lest it be concluded that all we have to do is to leave it all up to God! I am saying that grace is present in every situation, that the pattern of life-out-of-death is what Christians understand to be the pattern of every situation in life. But graces can be lost, opportunities can be missed, situations can be misunderstood. Hence there is a vital role for God's people themselves in discerning where the hope lies and in responding to the signs of hope in a given situation.

But in doing this, we have to submit ourselves to God's way of seeing things. An example of what I mean by this is St Paul (as reported by Luke) saying, as his imprisonment and death loomed on the horizon: 'I do not count my life of any value to myself, if only I may finish my course and the ministry that I received from the Lord Jesus, to testify to the good news of God's grace' (Acts 20: 24).

Only one thing matters to Paul, his ministry of testifying to what God is doing. His own preoccupations and preferences must give way to this. Applying this to ourselves, what matters is not how I see the situation or how you see the situation. What matters is how our God of hope sees things. What is demanded of us is that we leave all else aside in order to enter into God's way of seeing our situation.

Everything is Possible

I have said that what Christian hope asserts essentially is the sense of possibility in every situation. This sense of possibility is captured well in the film *Babette's Feast*, which won the Oscar for best foreign film in 1987.

The film concerns a small Lutheran community in the last century whose religion was very severe and puritanical, portraying an image of life and of God as hard and relentless. It tells of the transformation of this group, and of its faith, through the arrival of Babette and her presence amongst them, culminating in the feast she prepares. The analogy between Babette and Jesus, between the feast and the Eucharist, is clear.

My interest is in how the transformation is described. At an earlier stage of the story, the cavalry officer Lorens had seen his love for Martine, the Lutheran pastor's daughter, frustrated by the austerity of the pastor and his control over his daughters. As he leaves Martine, Lorens says to her: 'I am going away forever; I shall never see you again. For I have learned here that this life is hard and relentless, and that in this world there are things that are impossible.'

But he does see her again, some thirty years later, at the feast prepared by Babette, on the pastor's anniversary, for the now ageing and divided disciples. He is the one to put words on the significance of the grace worked by Babette in the group:

> We have all of us been told that grace is to be found in the universe. But in our human foolishness and short-sightedness we imagine divine grace to be finite. But the moment comes when our eyes are opened, and we realise that grace is infinite – grace, my friends, demands nothing of us but that we shall await it with confidence and acknowledge it with gratitude.

Long after midnight, as he is departing the feast, Lorens seizes Martine's hand, tells her that he has been with her every day of his life, and continues; 'and I shall be with you every day that is left to me; for tonight I have learned, dear sister, that in this world *everything is possible.*'

Learning to Hope

We have here a story of how Christian hope is learned. So often we set out with perspectives that in fact put limits on God's grace. But when 'our eyes are opened' we learn that grace is infinite, that everything is possible. We approach each situation with gratitude, confidence, expectation.

But I would emphasise that hope is *learned.* We in today's Church need to learn to hope because *we do not know much about hope.*

Hope thrives in adversity; it is most alive in troubled times and troubled minds. But our experience of Church until recently has not been one of adversity. We have grown up in what might be called a successful Church.

Perhaps that is why there is so little written about hope. We are not used to hope because we have not needed to hope. Therefore today, when times have changed, we find ourselves needing to learn how to hope. That learning begins, as I have been describing, by making contact with the God of hope.

ACKNOWLEDGING THE DIFFICULTIES

Everything is possible, but not everything is easy. Our tradition speaks of two sins against hope, the sins of presumption and despair. Presumption is a false confidence, even a smugness, about the future. It presumes that everything will be fine; it glosses over the difficulties. Despair, on the other hand, is overwhelmed by the difficulties and ceases to trust in the providence of God.

Hope negotiates between these two dangers. Its inspiration is the confidence that God's purposes are being achieved, but it acknowledges the difficulties that lie in the way. Therefore hope is essentially realistic. It is a combination of the desirable, the difficult and the possible. It can feel at the same time disappointment and expectation, frustration and excitement, anger and adventure, despondency and determination.

A Changed Context

Somebody once said: 'if you cannot be truthful about the life you have, you cannot hope for the life you want.' So, as Christian hope seeks to acknowledge truthfully the difficulties before it, what does it see? Perhaps more than anything, what it sees is *change*.

Even though it is now over thirty years since the Second Vatican Council, people are still talking about the changes in the Church. Usually this refers to the changes in the Mass, such as the priest facing the people, the use of English instead of Latin, the involvement of the congregation in ministry. It also refers to the demise of traditional devotions, such as benediction, rosary, sodalities, processions. More deeply, it refers to a changing sense of what religion is all about, a change from something quite church-centred to something life-centred.

We still talk about 'the changes' because many people are still coming to terms with them, most notably with the changing sense of what religion is all about. Yet, while all this is going on, I have a suspicion that 'the changes' are no longer the issue. It is not that Christians do not need to renew their understanding of what it means to be a Christian. But there has been a change in the context in which this is taking place. Amidst the changes within the Church and their assimilation by Christians, we are realising that something overarching has changed, something to do with the Church and culture.

A phrase comes to mind, which helps to understand this overarching change. It says: 'when everybody believes except the village atheist, then believing is easy.' The phrase captures well the situation of the Church in the middle of this century. Society was overwhelmingly Catholic; practically everybody 'practised'; there was no serious alternative to being a Catholic; the culture was supportive, shot through with religious meanings.

But nowadays the phrase might well read: 'when everybody

doubts except the village believer, then believing is difficult'! Of course things have not (or not yet) changed to quite that extent. Nevertheless there has been going on a most significant shift in the direction of the marginalisation of religion in our society. There is less and less that is smooth or automatic about becoming an adult Christian. There are serious alternatives. The culture is less and less supportive; sometimes it is quite hostile.

So, besides the issues of change within the Church, there is the overarching issue of the changing place of religion in society, moving from the centre to the margins, from a place of primacy towards a place of insignificance. This latter is the root difficulty facing renewal today, namely, the steady erosion of the very credibility and desirability of religion.

Something Gone – But What?

The difficulty is portrayed strikingly in Matthew Arnold's poem, *Dover Beach,* written in 1853. As the author looks out over the cliffs, the tide is full and the moon shines on the straits. He is drawn into reflection by 'the grating roar of pebbles which the waves suck back and fling, at their return, up the high strand, begin, and cease, and then again begin.' He reflects that 'the sea of faith' was once at full tide, but that now 'I only hear its melancholy, long, withdrawing roar'. He is left with a sense of something gone out of the world – a loss of certitude and light and peace – and he ends:

> And we are here as on a darkling plain
> Swept with confused alarms of struggle and flight,
> Where ignorant armies clash by night.

The poem well describes what we are experiencing in Ireland now – an unprecedented and, what seems to many, irreversible loss of religion and religious faith.

It is important, however, to measure the difficulties accurately. Something is gone, but what? Cardinal Newman said once that the Church can be mistaken to be in decline when it is only changing its form. Is this the case today? Is it that the trappings of religion are changed, but that the essentials are still intact? Is it that people are deserting a certain form of Church, or is it that religion itself is dying, and with it the sense of God? I will take up these questions in the next chapter.

GRASPING THE POSSIBILITIES

The Christian conviction, that everything works for the good for God's people, teaches us to look on all situations with eyes of hope, to be honest and realistic about the difficulties, while searching out the possibilities for rediscovering God and building God's Kingdom anew.

A Time to Explore

It was Enda Lyons who once said that, in a situation such as ours, four responses are possible. Firstly, we may *ignore.* We can bury our heads in the sand and hope that when we re-emerge the problem will have passed over. But it does not pass over and is still there when we look again.

So, instead of ignoring, we may *deplore.* We can say that the world is gone to the dogs, or that the Church is gone to the dogs, or that the children are no longer learning, or that the teachers are no longer teaching. But we eventually discover that deploring does not get us very far.

Then, instead, we may seek to *restore.* We can say, 'if only we could bring back the rosary, or the benediction, or the Corpus Christi procession, or the Latin singing.' 'If only…'. But we know in our hearts that the past is past and that there is no going back to the way things were.

So, when we know that it does not work either to *ignore* or to *deplore* or to *restore,* then it is time to *explore.* And that is the mood of hope. The times are difficult, but we trust the promise of Christ's abiding presence. We know that there are possibilities, paths leading forward out of the present, because God is at work. So, in a mood of hope, we explore to see which are the paths to follow. We seek out the signs of new life, we encourage the shoots of new growth.

Interestingly, as John Paul II says in his letter looking forward to the year 2000, these signs are not as obvious as it might seem:

> There is need for a better appreciation and understanding of the signs of hope present in the last part of this century, even though they often remain hidden from our ears.
> (*Tertio Millennio Adveniente,* paragraph 46)

Why do they often remain hidden from us? Perhaps it is because we are too attached to the Church as it has been. Perhaps we place our faith in the *forms* the Church has taken in the past, rather than in the enduring presence of God's Spirit through the *changing* forms of the Church. Perhaps we are too familiar with what has been the case to be able to appreciate what it is that is dying and what it is that coming to birth.

In fact, we need a dying and rising of our own, a conversion. We need to let go of our own assumptions and presumptions, our blinkered vision. We need to see anew or, as the bible puts it, to 'listen to what the Spirit is saying to the churches' (Revelation 2: 7). We need to see with something of God's own vision, detached yet passionate. If we learn to see thus, we begin to find signs of hope where we would not have expected them.

Blessing or Curse?

For instance, we might begin to see signs of hope in what would usually be seen as negative signs of despondency today – the fall in Mass attendance and the increasing absence from church of young to middle-aged adults; the near disappearance of vocations to the religious life and the priesthood; the scandals that have so damaged the church's credibility in recent years. If, as Christian hope insists, God's purposes are being achieved, then might there not be a blessing contained in these 'signs of the times'?

The reader may be familiar with a story of Anthony deMello, about an ageing farmer living on the side of the mountain and dependent on his one horse to do the heavy farmwork for him. One night in a storm the horse bolted and ran off into the mountains; the farmer was minus his means of livelihood.

The neighbours came round and sympathised with him on his bad luck. 'Good luck, bad luck; who knows?' was his philosophical reply. Within a few days the horse returned with another twenty wild horses it had met in the mountains. The neighbours called to congratulate the farmer on this piece of good luck. 'Good luck, bad luck; who knows?' was once again his reply.

The following day his son was thrown off one of the wild horses as he tried to break the horse in. As he lay in bed with a broken leg, again the neighbours called, sympathising with the farmer on this piece of bad luck. And again the farmer responded; 'Good luck, bad luck; who knows?' A week later, with the country at war, the army came to the village to conscript all the young men. When they saw the son in bed, they passed on. And the neighbours called... and the father replied...

The fact is, and our own experience confirms this, that often we do not appreciate the true significance of events while we are in the middle of them. What seems 'bad luck' may turn out, in retrospect, to have a quite different significance. I recall a friend's misery at having to go abroad for a number of years – and how he looks back on it now as one of the most worthwhile experiences of his life. Again, there are many who look back on times of pain and suffering as times of grace, because they now see the growth that was made possible.

And, indeed, this is what many people are beginning to detect in today's dark times for the Church, that there is a blessing in what seems only a curse. Perhaps the fall in Mass attendance is challenging us to rediscover a living worship that speaks to the lives of all God's people. Perhaps the disappearance of vocations is a call on parishioners to share the responsibility for the life of the Christian community. Perhaps the scandals of recent years are inviting us to replace clericalism with a more egalitarian and participative style of Christian community.

New Shoots of Life

Besides the hopeful possibilities contained in the seemingly negative, there are more positive signs of hope, new shoots of growth in the Church. But, again, if we are too attached to the forms of Church we have been used to, we may not be able to see these for the signs of hope that they are.

The signs of hope that I have in mind particularly here are all about the people of God. What I am saying is that the people of God are themselves *the* sign of hope in today's Church. This is evident in a number of ways.

There is the phenomenon today of a substantial and growing body of adult Christians who have become formally educated in their faith through participating in various theological courses. It used to be that the priest was looked up to as the educated person in the parish. But now more and more parishes are blessed with adults who are literate and articulate in areas such as theology, catechesis, liturgy and prayer guidance. These people constitute a very significant potential for pastoral leadership in the Church.

More generally, there are the new emerging forms of involvement of God's people in the life of the Church and the parish. In a vast array of ways, the giftedness of parishioners is being brought to bear on the quality of parish life. In the process more and more people are rediscovering what it means to be a member of the Christian community.

All of this is also revealing that there is a huge amount of energy and commitment for the work of renewal among God's people themselves. Whatever one thinks about the 'vocations crisis', there is no lack of 'labourers for the harvest'. No longer need the priest feel he must bear the burden alone. There are many who are willing and able to assume their share of the responsibility for their own future as God's people.

This brings us to what has been called 'the hour of the laity'. In previous times, it was figures such as the monks or the theologians or the missionaries who witnessed to God's continuing providence. Today, it is men and women in their parishes, entering with the priests into a shared responsibility for the life and future of the Christian community. This is the heart of parish renewal.

At the Synod on the Laity in 1987, Cardinal Tomás Ó Fiaich spoke of *the sleeping and now awakening giant* that is the laity, the people of God. The image is compelling. If one were to add up the number of people in the two hundred parishes of the Dublin diocese who are committed, involved, well-disposed, concerned for their Church, how many would there be? One hundred in each parish? One thousand or more in some parishes?

It is impossible to be exact. But let us guess. Let us say that in the two hundred parishes of the Dublin diocese, there are 50,000 people concerned for and committed to the future of their Church. Is that not cause for amazement? If we wonder what God is doing in today's situation, let us pay attention to this awakening giant.

Patience

This is but an indication of the signs of hope that are present. Some might think that it does not amount to much – perhaps because the impact so far has not been great. But it is a question of significance, not size. Recall what Jesus said about the mustard seed.

A more familiar image than the mustard seed is that of the acorn, which has been taken in the Dublin diocese as a symbol for the planning that is going on in the parishes for the next millennium. Like the mustard seed, the acorn's immediate impact is minimal – nothing in comparison to the ultimate significance of the oak tree. The acorn speaks of small beginnings, full of promise.

The image teaches us something important about the challenge to hope in today's Church. It teaches us that hope is about the long term and the long haul. Hope is based on a conviction about God's presence and providence, and on this basis it perceives the signs of hope in the present situation. But it knows that building on these signs is a gradual process. Therefore it is patient and confident.

> The farmer waits for the precious crop from the earth, being patient with it until it receives the early and the late rains. You also must be patient (James 4: 7-8).

A patient disposition is characteristic of hope, because hope is about that which is both desirable, difficult and possible. If it were not desirable and possible there would be no point waiting. If it were not difficult there would be nothing to wait for. But because it is difficult yet possible and desirable, it is worth waiting for.

Part of this patience is the realisation that we are not planting for ourselves, but for our children and our children's children. We plant some seeds today; we see some shoots; but we may not see much of the results. It may be generations before the full significance of what is beginning today is appreciated.

Resources

Themes of this Chapter	**Resource Material in Vol II**
Change in the Church.	*Called by Name,* session one. *From Maintenance to Mission,* session one.

CHAPTER 3

The spiritual hunger in people

In the last chapter I quoted Cardinal Newman to the effect that sometimes the church is thought to be in decline when it is only changing its form. And I asked, what is changing today, the trappings or the essentials? What is dying, a certain form of church or religion itself?

The question brings to mind promises made by Jesus. 'And remember I am with you always, to the end of the age' (Matthew 28: 20); 'And I tell you, you are Peter, and on this rock I will build my church, and the gates of Hades will not prevail against it' (Matthew 16: 18). There is something that remains, something with the permanence of rock, something foundational, but what is it? In what way does Jesus continue to be present?

The present chapter offers a way of thinking about these questions. It does so by elaborating on the distinction between 'spirituality' and 'religion'. It is a distinction that helps us see more clearly how God is working for the good in our situation today. This in turn provides a basis for the discussion in subsequent chapters of the meaning of the parish and of parish renewal.

SPIRITUALITY AND RELIGION

I recall reading an account of a survey carried out in Britain; obviously the details will be different in Ireland, but it is the overall point that matters. When asked if they went to church regularly, less than one in ten people said 'yes'. When asked if they had a personal spirituality, two out of three said 'yes' (*The Tablet*, March 2nd, 1996).

These figures represent in a striking way what research has repeatedly shown, namely, that non-practice of religion is not the same as loss of belief. There are many more people 'spiritually active' than appear in church on Sunday. It is on this basis that a distinction is made between 'spirituality' and 'religion'.

The word religion, in its current usage, tends to refer to organised religion, to a Church with its belief system, its code of behaviour, its rituals and observances (the 'creed, code and cult'). The word spirituality, on the other hand, has to do with something more inward and personal. It is about people's sense of the divine and their quest for meaning.

While I will stay with this usage, I realise that it is but one current usage. Sometimes the word religion is used to denote what I have described as spirituality. Indeed the virtue of *religio* in the Catholic tradition can be seen to refer to both religion and spirituality.

Perhaps the main difference is that, in today's usage, the word religion often has a negative sense, while the word spirituality in contrast refers to something positive. The question then arises; what is negative about religion? Many would reply that the word suggests authoritarianism, a restriction on freedom, condemnation and guilt, something that is behind the times and out of touch with reality.

For others it is that religion is something apart from life. I think of the man who interrupts himself in the middle of a conversation about religion to protest, '... now don't get me wrong Father, I'm not religious myself'! The protestation suggests that religion is about being 'holy' and that being holy is the calling of some and not all of God's people.

But the most significant negative association of the word religion is that it is seen by many as failing in its task of nourishing the person's spirituality. Many experience religious practices, most notably the Sunday Eucharist, as failing in this way. If others take exception to this, it is because their experience is different. In other words, people are quite happy with the word religion to the extent that their experience of it is that it nourishes their spirituality.

Thus it is often noted that the problem facing parish renewal is not to do with people's sense of God. It is to do with their sense of Church. By and large people have some sense of the divine in their lives. But many say that when they go to Mass on Sunday, it does not address this sense, it fails to touch into and enhance their awareness of God.

Again, those who are happy with their religion will find this hard to understand. Nevertheless there must be something amiss if this is the complaint of an increasing number of people.

Different Paths

It is worth reflecting for a moment on what happens subsequently to those who cease to 'practise' for reasons such as these. Some will continue to pray in their own way, but apart from the gatherings of the community. In others the spiritual sense will go dormant. Perhaps it will be awakened again by some future experience, perhaps not. In others, the resentment of religion will make it difficult for them to get back in touch with their own spirituality.

Others again will be vulnerable targets for religious cults. For, while they have stopped going to church, they are still open to God and, perhaps unconsciously, continue to desire some opportunity to renew their relationship with God. So, when the knock comes on the door, there is a willing audience. The Church would do well to reflect on this, that the cults thrive on people who have become dissatisfied with their own religion.

Finally, there are those who will move into an alternative spirituality. It may be creation spirituality, or Celtic spirituality, or a justice spirituality, or a charismatic spirituality, or a new age spirituality, or whatever. Some of these alternatives are themselves Christian, some only tenuously so, some not at all. But frequently it is the case that, while the person's spirituality is now being nourished in this new way, it is not bringing that person any closer to the religion that he or she left.

I think here of one woman who had long since given up going to church. Through participation in a personal development course her sense of God, her spirituality, was re-awakened. She loved to pray and to pray with others, but there was no way she would go back to church on Sunday. Increasingly, there are many like her.

Again, there is something here for the Church to reflect on as part of the agenda for renewal. The implication would seem to be very clear that, if there is to be any re-engagement with people such as these, there will have to be some change on the part of the Church. They left because their expectations were disappointed and they will hardly return to the same situation. But here I am anticipating a topic that will be taken up in chapter six.

What Endures?

At any rate, I began with a question; what is it that is changing or dying, and what is it that endures? My response is that what is foundational is spirituality and its need to find some expression in what we call religion. Spirituality is intrinsic to the person, part of what a person is. While the forms of religion change, this is what endures. Thus John Paul II, writing about the vocation and mission of the laity, says:

> Human longing and the need for religion are not able to be totally extinguished... the present-day world bears witness to this, in ever-increasing and impressive ways, through an openness to a spiritual and transcendent outlook towards life... the return to a sense of the sacred and to prayer, and the demand for freedom to call upon the name of the Lord. (CFL, paragraph 4)

Jesus promised to be with us always; but he is present as Spirit. The gift of the Spirit is the abiding form of Jesus' presence with us. And it is this presence that is testified to in people's own abiding spiritual sense. I said in the last chapter that parish renewal is grounded in the conviction that God's purposes are being achieved. Now it may be clearer how this is so. God is present, God is at work, in the Spirit of Jesus present in God's people. It is to the spirituality of people that we must look in order to see how God's will is being done today.

WHAT IS SPIRITUALITY?

While the word 'spirituality' is central to the present discussion, it remains an elusive word, used in many different ways. Therefore it will help to elaborate further on what it might mean.

As I understand it, spirituality is something that *all people* can recognise in themselves. Because each person is intrinsically and essentially spiritual, spirituality is for everybody. The man I mentioned above may not want himself described as 'religious', but I am sure he would accept that he is a spiritual being in the meaning intended here.

What is off-putting for many about words like 'religious' and 'spiritual' is a suspicion that they have to do with something other than the human, something 'set apart'. So it is important to emphasise that, while the words obviously have a transcendent reference, spirituality is primarily about *becoming more of a human being*. Spirituality does indeed refer to God, but as part of a search or process or journey where the person 'circles in' on his or her own true self. This is part of what Jesus meant when he spoke of people 'finding' or 'losing' their lives or souls.

An Illustration

A striking illustration of this is the experience which Brian Keenan recounts in his book, *An Evil Cradling,* about his horrific captivity in Beirut. He talks about the group of them imprisoned, all so different, nothing in their life histories that should have brought them together. 'We were all in our own way innocently walking over a bridge that had collapsed and we had all tumbled down here into this hole in the ground and found ourselves together. Why?'

He continues. In the long hours of talk and mania and contemplation, their 'minds having been pushed through all sorts of dark mysterious places', there was a single common denominator that emerged again and again – 'our relationship to and understanding and experience of love underlay everything else'.

> We each of us had fallen down into meaning, if we cared to seek it out, and to climb with it out of that awful chasm into which we had been toppled. The experience of love was the stepladder up which we could climb. (pages 270-271)

This *is* spirituality. It is about people finding themselves. It is about real, flesh-and-blood human experience. It is about the depth and meaning and mystery of that experience. It is saying that human experience is sacred.

The 'More' in Life

The example of Brian Keenan is a very dramatic one, so a few more 'for instances' may help to communicate the broader relevance of spirituality. The following 'for instances' are moments when people are 'spiritually active', moments when there is more, moments that testify to our spiritual nature. They may be less dramatic but they are no less real. For instance:

- A parent talking with her or his child at night.
- Moments of being together as a family.
- The man who spoke of the 'long and painful journey' from the God of fear to the God of love.

- The experience of being at one with nature or creation.
- The surfacing to consciousness of a passionate concern for the environment.
- The transcendence of the experience of love and commitment.
- The experience of being loved and lovable, of discovering within ourselves the spark of something we can like.
- The experience of being forgiven in the depths of our being.
- A moment of self-knowledge.
- Being brought out of ourselves by the suffering of another.
- Moments of tragedy or of ecstasy in society.
- The experience of taking on a responsibility.
- The awakening of our sense of justice; the mystical experience of the face of God in the poor.
- Being touched by the death of another, or reflecting on the prospect of our own death.

These are only 'for instances'; a few more voices and the list would be greatly enriched. But they do expand our idea of what spirituality is. It is about the 'more' in life, about the fact that there is more to life than meets the eye, something we call 'mystery'. It is not necessary that people use the word 'God'; they may even feel content without 'religion'. Most of the time that people are spiritually active they are not using religious language at all. They are talking about their dreams, their hopes, their concerns, their fears, their joy.

Nor does spirituality imply being very well educated in the formal sense. It is about being in touch with the inner self and with truth, goodness and beauty in the world. These discoveries are available to any person. Often books are an obstacle rather than a help. The truth is that, just as none of us escapes the burdens of life, so too each of us can enter into the depth of life's meaning.

Our spirituality is our sense that there is more to life. But it is also our sense that there is more to each of us ourselves. Jesus referred to this when he said that he had come that we might have life and have it to the full (John 10: 10). To live fully is to live at greater depth, more from the true 'me' than the superficial me. As I said earlier, spirituality is about the inner journey, circling in on the truth of ourselves.

Again, the 'for instances' tell us that spirituality is about our relationship to the whole. To be spiritually active is to have become conscious in some way of our relationship to the whole of reality. It is about taking a stance vis-a-vis the universe. It is about our interpretation of the meaning of life, by which we live our lives. It is about our contending with the great questions of who we are and what it is all about.

In this light of all this, it is perhaps more accurate to speak of spirituality as something we are rather than something we have. To say 'I have a spirituality' sounds a little like 'I have a theory' (about the meaning of life, or whatever). The truth, rather, is that I am in my very essence inescapably spiritual. To deny this would be to deny myself.

Both ... And ...

There are a few final points to be made before moving on, each in the form of a 'both-and'. Firstly, spirituality is bodily as well as spiritual, although it sometimes sounds as if it is not. It is not a denial of the body or a flight from the body. Rather, we are 'embodied spirits', so that spirituality includes being in touch with our bodies and being at home in our bodies.

Secondly, spirituality is worldly as well as transcendent. This created world is also part of what we are. We are creatures of planet earth, in fellowship with all living being. Rather than 'fleeing the world', true spirituality is a growth into an ever more harmonious interaction with the created world.

Thirdly, spirituality, while it is intensely personal, is not private. It is both personal and public. It concerns life in the world, the quality of our relatedness to others and of our life together on this planet and beyond. Therefore spirituality cannot be divorced from the public and the political. Unfortunately, some contemporary manifestations of spirituality are very privatised, concerned with 'the inner journey' and nothing more. This point leads us into the next consideration.

SPIRITUALITY AND CULTURE

I have said that the experience of many people today is that their 'religion' is not nourishing their 'spirituality'. But when it comes to the relationship between culture and spirituality, the situation is more serious still. What I have in mind here is the extent to which aspects of the culture we are a part of today do a disservice to spirituality and exert a destructive influence on the spiritual lives of people. If some of what follows seems exaggerated it is in order to communicate the importance for spirituality of what is involved.

Buying and Selling

I wish to focus on two aspects in particular. One is the *commercial* dimension of contemporary culture, the degree to which life today is driven by commerce and exchange, by capitalism. Today human relationships are being reduced more and more to the level of commercial transactions. Life is being taken over by the activity of buying-and-selling.

This may be quite evident but a couple of illustrations will not be out of order. On Irish television, *The Late Late Show,* which has been running since the early 1960s, used in its earlier years to be a chat show, with entertaining and often thought-provoking discussion and debate.

Now it is more accurately described as a two-hour advertising slot. If a guest is being interviewed, usually he or she has just published a book or is about to appear in concert in Ireland. If a group perform, they have just released a new CD. If there is 'one for everybody in the audience', the donor is getting prime time advertising space. One wonders why there are still 'commercial breaks' during the programme!

Sport is another illustration. Manchester United command a

great following in Ireland, but when we take in the full picture we see that sport is only a minor element. The turnover at the Old Trafford turnstiles is nothing compared to the turnover from parents paying out substantial sums for Man. Utd. gear for their youngsters. And it is nothing compared to the money changing hands in pubs thanks to Sky's exclusive rights to television coverage. This is but one of the more notable ways in which sport, once engaged in for its own sake, is becoming at its core a facade for huge commercial transactions.

Buying-and-selling is what life has come to mean, and in the process commerce has replaced religion as the 'glue' that is holding society together. Some centuries ago, Christianity was the common denominator and the common source of meaning in society. That is no more; capitalism has taken its place.

We see this reflected in the way the world of commerce has appropriated to itself the language of religion. Businesses produce 'mission' statements. Advertisements feed on the language of religion – a chocolate bar is 'paradise'; 'happiness' is a cigar; a mobile phone promises 'freedom'. We can smile at this of course, but it also represents a huge shift of meaning and value.

I mention all this because of what it is doing to persons. The reduction of so much human interrelating to commercial transactions means that the individual person is being seen more and more as *simply a consumer*. The more persons are viewed as consumers, the less they are cared for as persons. The language of 'customer care' means at most an enlightened form of self-interest whose care is ultimately for what is in the customer's pocket.

It cannot but be significant that the world we live in is pervaded by an ethos that does not care for us as persons, and where the strongest interests are ones that have no hesitation in manipulating us for the sake of profit. The extent to which we go along with the world we live in is the extent to which we lose touch with our spirit.

Privatisation

The second aspect of contemporary culture I wish to focus on is that of *privatisation*. Privatisation is part of capitalism, as we saw with the conservative government of the 1980s in Britain. But the privatisation I intend here is the privatisation of religion and morality – which itself has not a little to do with the dominance of capitalism, making as it does for the elimination of some potential critics from the public sphere.

This privatisation of religion has been going on for as long as commerce has been replacing religion as the underpinning of society. In the process, over the last few centuries, religion has been relegated more and more to the private sphere. The real world is the world of economics and politics, the world of profit and power. Religion is something optional. Individuals or groups may find some comfort in it amidst the harsh realities of life in the real world. It may give them the hope of some better world in the future. But it is marginal, like carriages on a siding in the train station.

Likewise, morality has undergone a privatisation. When religion ceased to be the unifying force in western society, the common basis for morality was also lost and nothing has taken the place of religion. With no common basis for morality, no common standard for right and wrong, no common vision of the good life, people have begun to speak of morality as their own 'private affair', a question of personal discretion. What is right for me is right for me; what is right for you is right for you. We each follow our own instinct, while making sure to tolerate and not hurt one another.

We end up living in two worlds. On the one hand there is the big impersonal world out there, the world of commerce, of economics and business. On the other there is my private world, the world of my own opinions and beliefs and values. And there is little or no link between the two. Again, the proliferation of privatised forms of spirituality only deepens the divide.

The Costs

Now, the privatisation of religion and morality is not without its advantages. It means that they are no longer imposed, or simply the result of conditioning, but freely chosen instead, the genuine expression of inner conviction. But this may not be as significant as what has been lost.

The relegation of religion and morality to the private realm means that we find ourselves living in a world where the most important questions of all are not discussed! As a colleague of mine put it, it is a world in which the most fundamental human questions are reflected upon almost exclusively in private, a world which implicitly tells people that their deepest fears and their highest hopes are best kept to themselves.

The questions that really matter, the 'spiritual' questions – who am I? why do I exist? what does it mean to be a human person? how can I be more of a human person? what does life mean? what is the good life? what can we hope for? is the universe on our side? is there something greater than ourselves? – these are questions that do not matter in the public world of commercial exchange. They have nothing to do with 'profit'.

Thus there is a yawning emptiness at the heart of our society. This cannot but make people frustrated at the core of their existence. Whether that frustration comes to consciousness or whether it is played out in some indirect way is another matter. But I cannot but be deeply affected for the worse if the most important dimensions of my existence in the world are systematically by-passed by the society in which I live.

As I said above I have sketched the situation in a black-and-white manner, in order to emphasise a trend, the way things are going in our society. The outcome is that what I have been calling spirituality is being smothered and not allowed to breathe. One thinks of what Jesus said about 'profit': what does gaining the world profit us if we lose our very selves?

THE MEANING AND PURPOSE OF RELIGION

It is commonly said that the Church is in crisis today, for reasons such as those referred to in the first chapter – falling attendances, the drying-up of vocations, the scandals that have eroded credibility – and also for the further reason reflected upon in this chapter – the failure of organised religion to nourish the spiritual hunger of many.

But the more serious crisis is that affecting spirituality, not Church or religion. Religion and Church are secondary. They do not exist for their own sake, though often they behave as if they do. Religion is not meant to be church-centred, but spirituality-centred and person-centred. It exists so that spirituality may be deepened, that God may be known, that people would thereby become more fully human. The usual way of putting this in theology is to say that the Church exists, not for itself, but for the sake of the Kingdom of God.

So it is spirituality that is in crisis, and for two reasons. The first is that it is not being adequately served by Church and religion. The second is that it is being suffocated by the capitalist ethos of contemporary culture. The first might not be too tragic if people were finding alternative ways towards spiritual self-discovery and growth. But the second diminishes and even eliminates that possibility for very many people.

The challenge to the Church, to organised religion, is clear. Its task is to address itself to the spiritual hunger in people and to speak to people about how the Christian gospel offers a 'way' (the original word for Christianity) for their spiritual quest. Its task is to renew itself as a 'midwife' to the spiritual. But it must carry out this task as a prophetic activity, challenging the suffocating effects of certain aspects of contemporary, capitalist culture.

A Focus for the Parish

In the next chapter I will consider the parish as a locus for this task. In a book about parish renewal, it has taken some time to arrive at a concentration on the parish itself. However, I hope it will be clear at this stage that it was necessary first to define the context in which the parish must operate today.

By way of conclusion to this chapter, I would suggest that a parish which sees its task along these lines is actually returning to its own roots in the gospel. For, long before the Christian religion became organised for life in the world, Jesus its founder focused his own ministry on nourishing and building up the human spirit, on leading people to a recovery of their humanity. His interest was *spirituality*, people becoming fully human as God created them to be.

The title of this chapter draws on the metaphor of hunger, but both the metaphor of hunger and the metaphor of thirst feature in Jesus' encounters in people. They occur almost alongside each other in John's gospel.

John chapter six recounts the event of the feeding of the five thousand. The next day the people come looking for Jesus again but, as he reveals to them, they are only looking for food that perishes. As he teaches them about spiritual hunger and the satisfaction that God gives, they say to him, 'Sir, give us this bread always.'

John chapter four recounts the meeting at the well of Jesus and the Samaritan woman. This time thirst is the theme and, parallel to the story of the bread, Jesus brings the conversation beyond physical to spiritual thirst, so that the woman says to him, 'Sir, give me this water.'

In both incidents, the story builds up to Jesus himself being the object of the hunger and thirst – Jesus himself being the living bread, the living water. That itself is not understood or accepted without a struggle, as we see in John chapter six where many of his disciples turned away and no longer went around with him.

Perhaps this tells us of two moments in the spiritual journey. One is where we come to see that our deepest desires are indeed spiritual. The other is where we come to see that Jesus himself is the object of our deepest desires. This may be a useful distinction to bear in mind in the context of parish renewal. Given our contemporary cultural context, we should not rush ahead too quickly to the second moment. Not too much can be taken for granted about the spiritual well-being of God's people in the world.

Resources

Themes of this Chapter	**Resource Material in Vol II**
Spirituality.	*Spirituality for Today* - a choice of twenty sessions offering resources for helping people continue their spiritual quest.
Spirituality and culture.	*From Maintenance to Mission,* session one.
Spiritual needs.	*Adult Religious Education in the Parish,* on the spiritual needs of people at different stages of life.

A Parish Renewal Mission also relates to the concerns of this chapter, insofar as the kind of Mission proposed begins by giving voice to people, inviting them to articulate something of their own spiritual experience, and then building the church-based stage of the Mission on what emerges from this.

CHAPTER 4

What the parish could become

The reflections in the last two chapters provide the context for focusing on the parish in chapters four, five and six. These chapters elaborate on a 'new mindset' for thinking about the parish that responds to the contemporary context. The present chapter articulates a vision of parish. Chapter five reflects on what it means to think of the parish in terms of mission. Chapter six goes on to outline some of the implications for pastoral strategy of the new mindset.

WHAT FUTURE FOR THE PARISH?

Is the Parish Obsolete?

A difficulty presents itself immediately; many people would see the parish as a thing of the past and not adequate to the challenge of satisfying the spiritual hunger of people today. Perhaps, they would say, the parish did fulfil this role in previous times, but times and circumstances have changed.

For one thing, mobility has become a very significant part of lifestyle, particularly in urban areas. People no longer spend their entire day around one geographical area. A person may live in one place, work quite a distance away, engage in leisure pursuits in another place again. There is no necessary link between the parish a person happens to live in and the place or group where that person experiences belonging and the fulfilment of participating and making a contribution.

Thus, the spiritual hunger in people is satisfied in a whole variety of ways today, many of which have little or no link with the parish as traditionally understood. It may even be the case that people find their needs satisfied through groups or processes that have nothing to do with religion at all.

Indeed, many would see the parish as part of 'religion', as that term was used in the last chapter. It is part of the organised religion which has failed to nourish them and which has alienated some of them. They see the parish as going about its own programme of activities in a way that does not seem to connect with their own spiritual needs. They see it as a carry-over from the past, not adapted to life in the contemporary world.

A Nuanced Reply

In this way the question is posed; is the parish obsolete? A nuanced reply is, I think, called for. From the point of view of the mission of the Church in the world today, there is little doubt but that the parish on its own is insufficient. Today's pastoral task requires a variety of initiatives. This is recognised by John Paul II when he says;

> Since the Church's task in our day is so great, its accomplishment cannot be left to the parish alone... There are many other places and forms of association through which the Church can be present and at work. All are necessary to carry out the work and grace of the gospel and to correspond to the various circumstances of life in which people find themselves today. (CFL, paragraph 26)

Parish renewal does not preclude but rather needs these other initiatives. These initiatives include:

- working with specific interest groups or age groups or need groups across different parishes, as is illustrated by the work of many diocesan agencies.
- neighbouring parishes co-operating on common interests – for instance, the parishes in Dublin's inner city addressing together the issues raised by the thousands of new apartments built in the area in recent years.
- the outreach of the Church through its participation in the country's educational system.
- availing of the mass media in order to communicate the gospel.

Notwithstanding all this, a key role remains for the parish. As the same paragraph of CFL continues, 'in our day the parish still enjoys a new and promising season'; it has 'an indispensable mission of great contemporary importance'. Significantly, however, the Pope goes on to say that this mission will involve the 'adaptation of parish structures... especially in promoting participation by the lay faithful in pastoral responsibilities' and the fostering of 'small, basic or so-called "living" communities.'

The reason why this is significant is that it means that the parish of the future will be different from the parish of the past. Those who would conclude that the parish is obsolete are doing so on the basis of the parish as it has been. Those who see a 'new and promising season' ahead for the parish are *thinking about parish in a new way.* This new way focuses on the idea of community.

SOCIETY ON A HUMAN SCALE

If the issue in our day is that of addressing the spiritual hunger in people, community is the response to that hunger. The rest of the chapter will be taken up with spelling out what is meant here by community. As will be seen, the term community is being used in a theological as well as a sociological sense.

A former prime minister of Britain is quoted as once saying that there is no such thing as society, that there are only individuals and families. In the light of the previous chapter it might be more accurate to say that there are only societies and individuals and that what is missing is something in between. On the one hand there is the large consumer society, dominated by buying and selling, growing more impersonal by the day. On the other hand there is the individual, cared for only as consumer, left to his or her private self as regards any deeper wants.

What is needed, clearly, is society on a human scale, and that is what I mean by the word 'community'. Community means society on a scale where persons can be persons. It is society on a scale where persons can be acknowledged in the fullness of their personhood and where they can therefore give expression to the full dimensions of themselves. In community, the person is not just a consumer; he or she is an embodied spirit. The person can be all that a person is.

Such is what a parish is meant to be today. In saying this I do not mean that it is the only such community. For such community takes a variety of forms today, through which people overcome the frustration of modern society and find fulfilment at the deeper levels of themselves. Nevertheless, while acknowledging this, the parish may be unique or almost unique among such communities.

The Great Questions

When we think about it, there are very few places that do what a parish does, or at least what a parish can do. Where else in modern society can people acknowledge that they are mortal? Where else can they explore the feelings that attend the prospect of eventual death? Where else today can people confess that they are sinners and in need of a word of forgiveness? Where else can they ask whether there is mercy in the universe? Where else can they find what Dag Hammerskjöld called 'something to live for, great enough to die for'?

Where else, in a world that glorifies beauty and vitality and prosperity, is brokenness given pride of place? Where else is the healing and making whole of persons such a priority? Where else are the mysteries of suffering and evil accepted and confronted? Where else, in our classified, segregated world, can rich and poor, educated and uneducated come to the same table with equal status? Where else can people give voice to their greatest doubts and put words on their deepest yearnings?

In other words, the parish is one of the few places where the most important questions in life, the very questions privatised in our contemporary culture, can be asked and acknowledged publicly. Who am I? What does it mean to be a human person? What can we hope for? It is one of the few places that acknowledges and addresses people in the fullness of their personhood, one of the few places that responds to the spiritual hunger in the human person.

But what is specific and distinctive about the parish is not simply its acknowledgment of the fullness of the person, for that may happen in other contexts too. What is distinctive is its bringing the spiritual hunger of people into communication with the gospel of Christ. It is not just that the parish recognises the person as spirit, but that it offers people, in and through the gospel, a way of exploring their spiritual journey and satisfying their spiritual hunger.

Still, it will be objected, this is unreal. This does not correspond to the kind of parish many are familiar with. 'Parish' for many suggests a geographical territory, an administrative unit. It suggests a structure, centred on the church building and the clergy and the services they provide. It suggests large numbers, far too big to allow for the experience of what we call 'community'. It suggests little in the line of a sense of belonging. It has little connection to life as it is lived in the ordinary world of everyday.

And again the reply is nuanced. Yes, this is what parish has often been and what many (maybe even most) parishes largely are today. But it need not be so and in a growing number of parishes it is not an accurate description of what is happening. For something new is happening in parishes. It may as yet be little more than an acorn, but it is no less significant for that. Perhaps, then, it might be better to translate the positive picture of the parish just presented into the terms in which it is actually being articulated by people in parishes today.

A NEW VISION OF PARISH

Frequently, when parishes are engaged in the process of renewal, people and priests come together to compose a statement expressing their hopes for their parish. These go by the name of 'vision statements' (when what is expressed is a general hope for the future) or 'mission statements' (when what is expressed is an objective to be pursued over a determinate period of time).

Obviously, the main value of such statements is for the people involved in composing them, as they are the people whose views they represent. Perhaps, indeed, the process of reaching the final statement, with the mutual learning and coming together it involves, is more significant than the statement itself. But when we look at a number of these statements, from a wide range of parishes, we can see many points in common.

It is these common elements that constitute the new understanding of parish today, the way in which people in parishes are 're-visioning' what parish is all about. Let us reflect, then, on these outstanding elements.

Hospitality

The first outstanding element in how people see their parish today has to do with *welcome*. Parishioners want their parishes to be places of hospitality, where people feel welcomed and appreciated, where people feel they belong. Many, as we know, feel excluded for one reason or another. They feel themselves to be on the outside looking in.

Those involved in parish renewal want, rather, that all God's

people in the parish would feel included, without pressure. They desire that people would feel about the parish something of what they feel about home, namely, that it is theirs and that they are welcome always. They want a parish where people experience toleration and acceptance. They want a parish where difference is celebrated, just as St Paul gave us the image of the human body, all of whose members are appreciated (1 Corinthians 12)

Parishes put this vision into action in a variety of ways, such as a ministry of hospitality at the Sunday Eucharist, or a welcoming team to visit new parishioners, or initiatives to reach out to those who feel alienated or have been hurt by the Church. As they do, they make real the words of John Paul II concerning the parish:

> ... its fundamental vocation and mission... to be a 'place' in the world for the community of believers to gather together ... to be a house of welcome to all and a place of service to all, or, as Pope John XXIII was fond of saying, to be the 'village fountain' to which all would have recourse in their thirst. (CFL, paragraph 27)

Note again the theme of the spiritual thirst. But people will not come to have their thirst quenched without being invited. The word must go out in the parish that all are welcome.

Loved by God

A second outstanding element in how people see their parish today is a deeper aspect of this sense of welcome and belonging. In being welcomed in the parish people feel they are *welcomed by God*. Today's parish is one where people have a deep sense of being loved by God. They know the dignity of being baptised. CFL speaks of this when it says: 'Rising from the waters of the Baptismal font, every Christian hears again the voice that was once heard on the banks of the river Jordan: "You are my beloved ..."' (paragraph 11).

This sense of being loved by God will be communicated through the welcoming, hospitable, inclusive nature of the parish. More specifically, it will be communicated through the face of God presented by those who preach the gospel and preside over the sacraments. That face of God will be a face of acceptance rather than condemnation, of healing rather than punishing, of future possibilities rather than past failures.

If this is in fact communicated, people can come to a new awareness and assurance of God's presence in their lives. As this happens, it frees people to live together in a new way where it is clearly manifest that the gospel is indeed 'good news' for God's people.

Togetherness

A third element identified by parishioners is *togetherness*. Today's parish is not a place for an individualistic 'me and Jesus' kind of spirituality, where people are too taken up with saving their own souls to be much concerned with anybody else. Parishioners

> can never remain in isolation from the community, but must live in a continual interaction with others, with a lively sense of fellowship, rejoicing in an equal dignity and common commitment to bring to fruition the immense treasure that each has inherited. (CFL, paragraph 20)

This togetherness is expressed most notably in an attentiveness to need. It is a further aspect of the sense of hospitality and of being loved by God, that people would feel cared for in all their needs. Today's parish strives to be a place where nobody suffers alone, but where fellow-Christians put the needs of each other before their own (Philippians 2: 4). It is a neighbourly place, with frequent demonstrations of the generosity of the human heart.

In such a parish people feel they are part of a community that loves them. There is a common bond of love whereby people feel confident of support, friendship and forgiveness. There is an

ethos of the 'good Samaritan', a real sense that people are responsible for each other.

Such an ethos challenges the privatising trend in our culture. It strongly resists the idea that we each inhabit a private world and that it is 'everybody for themselves'. It proclaims that we discover our vocation and destiny as human beings together and not alone.

A Living Liturgy

Fourthly, parishioners today identify *living liturgy* as an outstanding element in how they see their parish. Here, every Sunday, the welcoming, hospitable nature of the parish is visible and the sense of belonging is palpable. Eucharist is, after all, the highest expression of the meaning of Christian community. Therefore here more than anywhere should it be evident just what the parish is.

Such a Mass is the opposite of boring. Rather, it reflects all that makes up the daily lives of those present. People's lives and struggles are not left in the porch, as happens so often. Their concerns are brought up to the altar, prayed over and celebrated in Christ. In this way the spiritual hunger of people is satisfied; but also their thirst is whetted as they are encouraged in Christian living!

If such is the case, then liturgy really is what Vatican II called it, the source and the summit of Christian living. The word of God will be alive and active. People will know that the Lord is the wellspring of everything in their lives. There will be a deep sense of Christian values and of what it means to be a Christian. And the young will participate.

Giftedness

The final outstanding element which people seek in their parishes today has to do with *gifts and giftedness*. If in the past much parish activity revolved around what the priest did, but this will not be the case in the future. Today's parish is about a sense of participation and an active involvement on the part of all.

This too is an aspect of being welcomed and loved. In the context of such hospitality people are encouraged to believe in their own giftedness. People come to know that they are each 'unique and irrepeatable', that God calls 'each one personally by name', that each has a own unique contribution to make to the growth of the Christian community (CFL, paragraph 28).

In such a parish the rich variety of human giftedness will become apparent. People will be eager to play their part, as they see how indispensable their giftedness is in the building of God's Kingdom. They will appreciate that giftedness is not about the special skills or aptitudes of some but about the precious humanity of all, about people enriching each other through their ordinary-yet-extraordinary human qualities.

The Structure and the Experience

Thus we have a contrast – those who see parish as obsolete and those who see parish as just described. *The contrast is not between two theories, but between two experiences*, for both can be observed in the Church today. But one is the experience of the past, the other the experience of the future. The difference is often described in terms of a shift in recent decades from an institutional to a communal way of seeing the parish.

> The parish is not principally a structure, a territory, or a building, but rather, 'the family of God, a fellowship afire with a unifying Spirit', 'a familial and welcoming home', the 'community of the faithful. (CFL, paragraph 26)

To spell out what this shift means, imagine that you are a member of a social club – say a bridge club or a football club – and you are asked to describe your club. You could, on the one hand, speak about the terms of membership, the way the club is structured, with its committee and officers and elections, the constitution and the rules, the opening times and the holidays.

On the other hand, you might describe what being a member is like – (for instance), there are thirty-five of us; membership has been going up recently; great buzz every Tuesday; cup of tea to end the evening; annual outing; friends made.

One of these describes the structure, the other the experience. Many people, when they think of the parish, think of *structure* – the staff, the services, the rules. In this way parish is more to do with 'religion' than 'spirituality', and we can readily see how it might be found distant and uninviting. But others think of *experience* when they think of parish – of what it is like living here, of the welcome on Sunday, of the Christian spirit, of the neighbourliness, of services that nourish the spirit.

In this sense, I am not talking about different theories of what the parish is, or opting for one theory over another. Rather, I am identifying different ways people think about parish, emphasising in the process the way of thinking that is especially life-giving today, as one that is capable of delivering on the promise of nourishing the spiritual hunger in people.

BACK TO ROOTS

The Early Christian Community

Next I wish to place this reflection in a biblical context. This will indicate how close today's vision of parish is to the heart of the message of the New Testament. First, let us recall Luke's well-known depiction of the earliest Christian community:

> They devoted themselves to the apostles' teaching and fellowship, to the breaking of bread and the prayers... All who believed were together and had all things in common; they would sell their possessions and goods and distribute the proceeds to all, as any had need... the whole group of those who believed were of one heart and soul. (Acts 2: 42-44; 4: 32)

The parallels between Luke's description and the elements of the vision of parish being articulated today are striking:
(1) Luke's mention of the teaching of the apostles corresponds to the sense of being loved by God in the above. For the gospel of the love of God is the very heart of the apostle's teaching. (2) Luke's reference to fellowship corresponds to the themes of

welcome and belonging above.
(3) Where Luke speaks of the breaking of bread, I spoke above of the centrality of a living liturgy.
(4) Both the passage from Luke and the vision articulated above speak of an attention to and prioritising of those in need.

The correspondence is not exact, but it is very close. What the closeness suggests is, firstly, that there are core identifiable elements of Christian community, going back to the New Testament and, secondly, that today's process of parish renewal is bringing those elements to the fore again.

The Vision of Jesus

Not alone that, but what we are talking about is to be found at the heart of Jesus' own ministry. Scholars now recognise that one of the most characteristic aspects of Jesus' ministry was his association and table-fellowship with the so-called sinners and tax-collectors, the outcasts of society. Not alone does this simple action of Jesus encapsulate the significance of his whole ministry; it also includes within itself the various aspects of the contemporary vision of parish.

(1) Jesus' table-fellowship speaks welcome and hospitality. It says to those who have no place that 'this is your place'. It speaks belonging to those on the margins and out in the cold. But it is also a hospitality that is inclusive. This is confirmed by the various references in the gospels to Jesus' sitting at table with the Pharisees also. It is the inclusiveness of God's own love, nobody beyond the reach of its embrace.

(2) In and through this table-fellowship people come to a new sense of being loved by God. Through Jesus they hear the words, 'you are my beloved'. Before meeting Jesus they had heard nothing but the opposite. But now their personhood is established again; they rediscover their humanity. The hunger and thirst that they had almost forgotten about, so submerged were these by condemnation and rejection, are affirmed and satisfied. As a result, people can stand tall again.

(3) Table-fellowship releases gifts. As people rediscover that they are loved at the core of their being, they realise that they are lovable and able to love. The love blocked up through sin and rejection can flow freely again. Stories such as those of Zacchaeus (Luke 19) and of the sinner woman who washes

Jesus' feet with her tears (Luke 7) are eloquent testimony to this release of giftedness.

(4) It is noteworthy that the giftedness has to do with the capacity to love. This relates to the theme of togetherness and mutual care in today's vision of parish. Through releasing the giftedness in people, Jesus' table-fellowship returns people to the togetherness of community.

(5) Finally, table-fellowship is liturgy. Jesus' table-fellowship is intimately connected to the Last Supper and to the breaking of bread among his followers. Each is the same experience of his self-giving as food in our hunger and drink in our thirst, nourishing us on our spiritual journey.

A Parable of Parish

Word and deed go together in the ministry of Jesus. Thus his action of table-fellowship is matched by his imaging of the heavenly banquet, of which this fellowship is a foretaste. But, from the point of view of parish renewal, the 'word' that perhaps best captures the significance of Jesus' table-fellowship is the story of the prodigal son.

This may sound strange because we are used to listening to the story of the prodigal as a story about God, whereas I am proposing a further interpretation of it, as a story about parish. In this sense the story complements Jesus' action of table-fellowship, so as to be a story symbolising the meaning of parish.

In this interpretation there is also an element of dialectic, in that the father and the elder son in the story represent two possibilities for parish. The father stands for the parish that is shot through with the hospitality of God's unmerited love. The son, as he approaches feels the exclusion he has brought upon himself. But, whereas he is saying 'I am sinner', the father is saying 'You are son'. For this place is and always will be home. We do not know how things transpired after they sat at table together, but it can be presumed that there were new beginnings.

The elder son stands for a different kind of parish. His words are not words of welcome but words of judgment. Hospitality is reserved: 'he did this… therefore…' This carries no sense of being loved, no sense of togetherness, no sense of humanity rediscovered and giftedness released. At some level, of course, it is correct – the younger son did do wrong; we cannot condone any sort of behaviour – and we do feel sympathy for the elder son's perspective. But at another level it misses out completely.

I wonder if, when people today find it difficult to imagine parish in the way being proposed, they are not thinking of parish more along the lines symbolised by the elder son in the story? Again, it is understandable if that is the case and there are reasons why people think in this way. But something new is happening to the reality of parish, something rooted in the life and ministry of Jesus himself.

THE MYSTERY OF CHRISTIAN COMMUNION

There is one final stage to our reflection in this chapter. Not only does the contemporary vision of parish resonate with the heart of Jesus' ministry on earth; it also reaches into the heart of God. Here I wish to suggest how the vision of parish is rooted in the doctrine of the Trinity.

The doctrine of the Trinity, for all the mystery it contains, is expressed in three words of St John: God is love (1 John 4: 16). God is not the old man in the sky, or the judge-on-high, or any of the other inadequate, monadic images we have inflicted on God and on ourselves. *God is community*, an everlasting giving and receiving of love, an infinite loving and being loved. This is what the doctrine of the Trinity reveals to us.

But the Trinity is not something apart from ourselves. The reason we exist at all is that God wishes us to be part of God's self. We exist in order to be loved by God and to know what it is to be loved eternally. Our life on earth is our initiation into this destiny, the Spirit drawing us into the experience of being sons and daughters, in Christ, of the Father.

We enter into this destiny by creating on earth the kind of community where each person experiences what it is to be loved. Knowing what it is to be loved in Christian community is thus a sign and foretaste of our eternal destiny. Parish is the earthly form of Trinitarian existence.

This relates closely to two of our fundamental needs as human persons. On the one hand, we desire to be independent or autonomous, completely ourselves. On the other, we desire to belong, to be immersed in love. And we want both together, lest belonging smother our individuality and lest being independent leaves us isolated.

Christian community is about the two together, a completeness of love where we flower as the unique individuals we are. But such community is a reflection of and participation in the Trinity. There we find three divine persons, each completely distinct and all completely one. Parish community is a participation in the life of the Trinity to the extent that the unique giftedness of each is cherished within the unity and togetherness of all.

'Parish'

Something of this link between now and hereafter is actually contained in the word 'parish'. As used in the New Testament, the word from which our word parish derives (*paroikia*) has the sense *both* of dwelling nearby as neighbours *and* of dwelling abroad as a stranger. In particular, it has the sense of a temporary dwelling in which community is experienced. It is used, for instance, to denote the 'stay' of the Israelites in Egypt (Acts 13: 17). The person in this situation is then described as an exile, a stranger in a foreign land, a resident alien (Acts 7: 6, 29; 1 Peter 1: 17; 2: 11).

The parishioner, therefore, is somebody whose true home is elsewhere (as when Hebrews 13: 14 says that 'here we have no lasting city'). Following from this, the parish is to be a 'home from home', where God's people may know the truth that 'you are no longer strangers and aliens, but you are citizens with the saints and also members of the household of God' (Ephesians 2: 19). The community that Christians share is thus an anticipation of their Trinitarian destiny.

It is in this sense that 'community' for Christians is a theological and not just a sociological term. Because of the context in which it belongs, it refers to a mode of being together that is unique, without parallel in the world. For this reason Church documents prefer to use the word 'communion' or the Latin *communio.*

> The communion of Christians with Jesus has the communion of God as Trinity... as its model and source... In this communion is the wonderful reflection and participation in the mystery of the intimate life of love in God as Trinity, Father, Son and Holy Spirit. (CFL, paragraph 18)

The anticipatory character of Christian community is captured in our calling the Eucharist a 'foretaste of the paschal feast of heaven'. This brings to mind what is said at the close of the Jewish Passover: 'next year, in Jerusalem'. In similar fashion the Eucharist, the celebration of Christian community, looks forward to the 'new and eternal Jerusalem'. And it does so by carrying the liturgy into life, by going out from the Eucharist to create the homeliness for which all God's people hunger.

Another word for this is 'companionship' – literally, bread together. To break bread together is to be bread for each other in our spiritual hunger, on our spiritual journey, to our true home in the Trinity. It is to such companionship that the parish is called.

Resources

Themes of this Chapter	**Resource Material in Vol II**
Our vision of parish.	*Called by Name*, session four, where parishioners share their vision of parish.
Sharing our vision of parish.	*The Priest and Parish Renewal*, a series of meetings where the parish team share their vision of parish.
The parish as context for renewal	*The Core Group and Parish Renewal*, session two.

CHAPTER 5

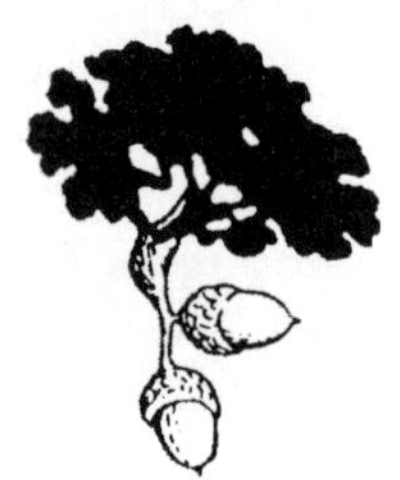

Focus on mission

The vision of parish articulated in the last chapter will have a broad appeal. However, this very appeal may obscure the change of mindset required on the part of priests, parish teams and parishioners in order to make the vision a reality. For the vision will not be realised simply by putting a greater effort into doing the things we have always been doing. A new way of seeing parish ministry is called for. That new mindset is what is referred to in the phrase 'from maintenance to mission'.

FROM MAINTENANCE TO MISSION

The phrase 'from maintenance to mission' has been current for some time now. It has become jargon and yet it refers to something of the greatest importance. But both words, maintenance and mission, have different meanings for different people. Therefore both require comment and clarification.

At its simplest, the shift from maintenance to mission means a shift from focusing effort on maintaining what is there already to focusing effort on striking out in order to put something different in place. In this the word 'maintenance' usually has a pejorative meaning. It tends to mean preserving the status quo, as if nothing had changed in the situation of the Church. It implies a failure to recognise the need for anything radically new.

Sometimes, for instance, priests refer to the 'parish plant' ('plant' in the factory rather than botanical sense). The phrase suggests that they sometimes see their role as largely a matter of maintaining certain structures, such as the church building, the services, the schools, the finances. This is confirmed by the amount of time and energy which priests have to invest in these responsibilities. But it is time which more and more priests feel is distracting them from their proper ministry.

There is much validity in the criticism of this 'maintenance' mentality, but there is also a sense in which criticism can be unfair. For any group, once it begins to become organised, requires maintenance. Be it the bridge club or the prayer group or whatever, some structure is needed. There has to be some form of leadership, some arrangement for meeting and for structuring meetings, some control of finances, and so on. Without such maintenance any group will fall into disarray.

In a somewhat different meaning, group theory also speaks of the ' maintenance needs' of a group. These include the need for members to feel accepted and appreciated, to know that their efforts matter, that their gifts are used, that they have a role to play. If all the energy goes into the tasks to be performed, so that these needs are forgotten, then the group will quickly run into trouble. It will have failed to maintain itself as a well-functioning group.

Keeping Things Ticking Over

However, the meaning of maintenance intended here is different. It emerges from an appreciation of the changes that have occurred in the Irish Church over the past half-century or so. Around the middle of the twentieth century, Irish culture was permeated with a Catholic ethos. Growing up as a Catholic was almost automatic, so strong was the socialisation process. It was a case of what I described earlier; when everybody believes except the village atheist, believing is easy.

The Church then could hardly have been in a stronger position. Some would say that it was too successful! I recall a friend recounting how, the year he finished secondary school – it was around 1950 – over half of the boys went on to the seminary. When today we bemoan the lack of vocations, we can fail to appreciate how inflated the number of vocations was back then.

No doubt not all was as it seemed to be. For instance, the huge numbers attending church included a number who were there simply due to the power of social controls, without any great inner motivation. Nevertheless, it can be said that overall the system was in good working order, at least externally. In that context the job of the priest was largely a matter of keeping things ticking over. He kept things going, providing the services year in, year out.

In other words, what the priest was doing was maintaining. It would have been similar to having a good car with no major dysfunctions. All such a car requires is periodic maintenance, servicing, polishing. Questions of overhaul do not arise. So the priest's job was to maintain a well-functioning system. Little changed from year to year. Roles were clear. Overhaul was not contemplated.

I have been trying to put this descriptively rather than critically. It is easy to look back and to criticise the past from the perspective of the present. It is not so easy to see the past from the perspective of the past. Thus, I am presenting the idea of maintenance as something that would have been quite normal, even positive, although the actual word maintenance would not have been used.

A New Situation

This is the way things were and this is how things were seen. But it is no longer adequate, because the system is no longer in good working order. As one priest bluntly put it, 'the system isn't working anymore'. Fewer and fewer attend church. The culture is less and less permeated by a Catholic ethos and now contains significant anti-religious elements. Growing up as a Catholic is far from automatic and can no longer be taken for granted.

There has been a lot of change. Priests and others responsible for parish life cannot continue to operate as if nothing had changed. It is not enough to continue to focus energy on providing substantially the same services as before and think that somehow that is going to bring people back. Things are not going to return to what they were.

To think like that would be similar to a parent reacting to a son or daughter running away from home, by doing nothing more than keeping the child's bedroom cleaned and dusted each day, as if that were going to bring him or her back. Unfortunately, however, many priests and parishioners continue to go on like that and refuse to acknowledge what has changed.

The diagram opposite represents something of the situation that pertains as a result. The large box stands for the kind of activities that would have been associated with the work of the priest in the past. Most of this activity would have centred around administering the sacraments and maintaining the parish.

SACRAMENTS

DEVOTIONS

SCHOOLS

FINANCES

FAITH FRIENDS
BEREAVEMENT GROUPS
TAIZË PRAYER

Pre-Evangelisation
Outreach

The smaller middle box stands for the various new pastoral initiatives that have been developed in recent years. The very fact of their existence says something about the need for renewal. They testify too to the inadequacy of persisting with the way things used to be done.

The smallest box stands for the very innovative projects that seek to reach out to those with whom the parish has lost contact. As yet they are only beginning and examples of them would be found only in a few parishes

The size of the boxes is proportionate to the amount of energy parish personnel (I am thinking mainly of priests) put into that area. Thus by far the greatest bulk of time and energy still goes into the traditional areas of activity. Some time and energy has been redirected into such initiatives as faith-friends, the GIFT programme, new forms of prayer, bereavement groups, baptism teams, and so on. As yet very little effort – none in most parishes – has been channelled into the area of evangelisation, re-evangelisation and pre-evangelisation.

This might not be a cause of worry, were it not that the size of the boxes is in *inverse* relationship to the number of people being touched by the effort. Here I am exaggerating in order to communicate a point. It is increasingly the case that less and less of the people in the parish are being touched by the efforts put into the first box. They are simply not there any longer. More and more of the people are in the second or even the third box.

In other words, time and energy are not moving with people. It is in this sense that I said above that the former situation no longer obtains and that it is futile to continue to operate as if it did. No amount of attention to the administration of the sacraments and to the traditional range of activities in which a priest was engaged is going to bring back those who have drifted away. Improving the quality of what is being provided will certainly have its place, but as part of a new strategy, not as part of the old. *There is need to think differently.* There is need of a new mindset.

THE MINDSET OF MISSION

This new mindset is what the word 'mission' refers to. The issue is captured well by John Paul II when he says:

> Without doubt a mending of the Christian fabric of society is urgently needed... But for this to come about what is needed is to first remake the Christian fabric of the ecclesial community itself... (CFL, paragraph 34)

This remaking of the parish will not come about simply by priests'providing the traditional services. It demands firstly that the parish itself be reconceived as *missionary territory*. It can no longer be presumed that missionary territory is somewhere else, on other continents. It is on our doorstep.

Thus the word mission is being used here in a new sense. In times past it meant bringing the gospel (and with it European culture) to foreign lands. More recently it has meant enabling the indigenous growth of local Churches in foreign lands. But our meaning is to see the parish at home in terms of mission or evangelisation. It is to acknowledge that the pressing need is not just the building up of faith in Christ, but the very awakening of such faith.

To accept that the parish is missionary territory is to recognise that growing numbers of baptised people are in need, not of catechesis, but of re-evangelisation. It is to recognise that for growing numbers of people there is little or no contact between their spiritual hunger and the gospel of Jesus Christ. It is to recognise that many people are not even in touch with the spiritual hunger within themselves.

Seeing Familiar Things Differently

Seeing the parish in terms of mission will mean the redirection of time and energy into new initiatives. But it will first of all mean reconceiving some traditional parish activities. In fact this has *already* been happening in most parishes. A mindset of mission is already implicit in the way we have started doing traditional things in a different way.

A good example of this is parish visitation. Visiting homes was one of the characteristic activities of the priest in the past. But nowadays parishes are thinking in terms of involving parishioners in this activity. Singly or in pairs, parishioners would go around to the homes. This might be as part of a hospitality team or a baptism team, or simply to generate new contact between individuals and the parish.

But in this way the traditional practice of visitation is being transformed into a missionary or evangelising activity. Its missionary nature is most evident in parishes where religious practice has fallen most sharply, or in the huge number of new apartment blocks in Dublin's inner city parishes. In these cases trying to make any kind of contact is itself a daunting task.

School ministry is another example of doing traditional things differently. Previously the priest visited the school to contribute to the school's catechetical work. But now such work has become a work of evangelisation, given that growing numbers of children receive no religious formation at home. In turn, sacramental preparation programmes (first communion, confirmation) are as much occasions for outreach and evangelisation as they are celebrations of faith.

Similar things could be said about baptisms and marriages and funerals. Previously part of the maintenance work of the priest, nowadays it is far more realistic to understand them in terms of mission. Many who attend baptism or marriage or funeral ceremonies do not otherwise come to the church. Therefore to treat these as routine occasions rather than see them as opportunities for outreach is to bury one's head in the sand.

New Forms of Ministry

Besides seeing familiar things differently, the mindset of mission involves the channelling of time and energy into new forms of ministry. This is what the diagram above indicates. In order to reach out effectively to all God's people, mission demands new initiatives and new styles of ministry.

Another way of putting this would be to say that the mindset of mission is inclusive in a way that maintenance generally is not. For the most part, maintenance only touches those who are still involved; most if not all its efforts are directed to them. It makes little or no impact on those who, for whatever reason, have ceased to participate.

The mindset of mission is also more people-centred, where maintenance tends to be more church-centred. Maintenance thinks in terms of the services provided and of the efficiency with which they are provided. But mission thinks in terms of the spiritual hunger of all the people in the parish, whether they partake of the services provided or not.

If what is being provided leaves many untouched, then new forms of reaching out will have to be devised. If God's people are not in the church, then they must be sought out where they are. It is the difference between a church-centred mission and a mission-centred Church. A mission-centred Church goes to where people are, to become familiar with their situation and to see where the connections are between their experience of life and the gospel.

Part of the significance of the presence of parish sisters has to do with this. Very often, the work of parish sisters brings them into contact with people who do not participate, in a way that the work of priests does not. While there are many other dimensions to their contribution to the parish, much of the work of sisters is about being with people in their situation in life. As such it is a witness to all in parish ministry of the new mindset already in operation.

All this is not meant to neglect the fact that some of the evangelising effort will be directed to those who continue to participate in the parish. Given the changes that have occurred, perhaps all Christians are in need of some form of re-evangelisation, in order that they can redefine their Christian identity in the new situation. Without this, it is probable that many of those who continue to participate will only be hanging on by a thread.

A NEW MINDSET FOR PRIESTS

Traditionally the priest has been to the fore in the life of the parish. In the future he will continue to be to the fore, but in a different way than previously. He will be to the fore in his promoting the mindset of mission. The *Directory on the Ministry and Life of Priests* (Vatican Congregation for the Clergy, 1994) leaves no doubt about the centrality of the priest in what it calls this 'new evangelisation'.

The document makes the important point that the work of priests is of a *changing* nature, that it must orient itself to the specific demands of the times. It continues:

> Thus it is clear that the priest is involved in a very special way in the effort of the entire Church to carry out the new evangelisation... In the new evangelisation, the priest is called to be the herald of hope... the priestly ministry is called to respond promptly and incisively to the search for

the sacred and for authentic spirituality which today is emerging in a particular way.' (paragraphs 35, 36)

Obstacles to Change

The reaction of many priests would be to say, 'I wasn't trained for this.' So it is understandable that the challenge provokes apprehension and fear. Most priests were trained for a form of Church that is no more and for a form of parish ministry that is no more.

They were trained to administer something that was running quite smoothly. This is true, not just of priests ordained in the 1950s, but also, I suspect, of priests ordained in the 1980s. While certain aspects of the training have adapted to the times, it has remained essentially training for work in a maintenance Church.

Priests often react by asking, 'will this mean more meetings?' Often this is meant sincerely. The demands of maintaining and servicing the parish as it is leave the priest being a 'jack of all trades', scattered this way and that. There are enough demands on his time already. He has become accustomed to working in certain grooves and finds it very difficult to leave them, or to envisage how he could leave them.

This point, of course, is true not only of priests in parishes, but of workers in any organisation that is contemplating serious overhaul. It is always very difficult to disengage from the demands of the job as it is, in order to address the demands of the job as it needs to be. The former demands impose themselves in a way that makes it very difficult to attend seriously to anything else.

Sometimes a 'fire-brigade' mentality is adopted. This mentality targets some one issue as being the crucial concern and then responds intensively to that issue, as if it contained a magic answer. It may be youth; it may be adult education; it may be prayer. Whatever it is, the point is that the emergency energy being invested is at the same time avoiding the need to reconceive parish ministry as a whole – the need for a shift in mindset.

For, once the emergency is dealt with, maintenance can continue as before. But the problem is not any single issue; there is no magic answer. The only answer is to undergo the change in mindset from maintenance to mission, allowing the Spirit to lead the way. *Change is the only magic answer.*

The Way Forward: Collaboration

Because of all this, maintenance persists when mission is needed. This often manifests itself in the priest continuing to do, and continuing to insist on doing everything himself, as he used to do in the past. At most he 'delegates' some tasks to others, but he cannot let go. As a result he feels snowed under without having even begun to address the challenge of mission. He finds himself 'so busy' and may even end up saying 'poor me' because of all the demands made on him.

What it is that he cannot let go of is an interesting question. Is it the parish as it used to be? Is it power and authority and, thereby, some sense of his own not being dispensable? Is it his identity as a priest? Is he afraid that if he lets go things will fall apart? Is he afraid of being inadequate and vulnerable?

Perhaps the main obstacle to transition on the part of priests is this tendency to think that it is all 'up to me'. It may have been true in the past that everything was up to the priest, but not now. Apart from anything else, the task is simply too great for this group of men, who are both ageing and declining in number.

It would seem, then, that even purely for pragmatic reasons, mission demands collaboration or co-responsibility between priests and parishioners. However, as will be seen in part two, the reasons for collaboration are not only pragmatic but also deeply theological.

One of the effects of collaboration is that it makes for a shift from task-oriented to people-oriented activity. Much maintenance activity revolves around parish structures – upkeep of premises and administration of finances for instance. For many priests this work consumes a lot of time and makes for much anxiety. It locks them into a very restricted form of ministry.

Collaborative ministry between priests and parishioners, on the other hand, releases people to attend to the issues of mission and evangelisation. The very experience of new partnership encourages people to take up a challenge that previously seemed too daunting. Also, because parishioners can share the burden of maintenance – in some aspects of which they are more competent anyway – the priest can be freed to redirect some of his time and energy to activity that is more distinctively *priestly* ministry.

It is clear, however, that if mission is to be taken seriously, serious retraining on the part of priests is necessary. This need will only be accentuated when we consider in more detail the demands which collaborative ministry makes on the priest. As priests themselves recognise, they were trained for something else. While openness and good will are invaluable in making the transition to a missionary consciousness, they will not be enough.

A NEW MINDSET FOR PARISHIONERS

'It's the Priest's Job'

Like the priest, parishioners are familiar with the parish as it has been and with their own role therein. If in the past the priest did everything himself, equally in the past parishioners were used to a passive role. When they are asked to change and to see themselves in a more active role in a mission-oriented parish, the frequent reaction is, 'but that's the priest's job'.

Sometimes today the parish church is compared to the supermarket. People come to get stocked up for the week ahead, but they can also shop around for better bargains elsewhere. In this comparison, the parish is not so much a community as a service that is available. It is up to parish personnel to make their offering as attractive as possible. The parishioner can take it or leave it or shop around elsewhere for a better service. But he or she remains in a receptive mode.

Of course this is not the attitude of every parishioner. But it is an extreme version of the mentality of many, namely, that 'parish' is about services that certain others provide *for* me. It is something which 'they' do. In this way parishioners themselves can feed the mentality of maintenance, where the priest does everything and provides the services, week in and week out.

A New Kind of Parishioner

But today there is emerging what might be called a new kind of parishioner. One manifestation of this is the growing number of parishioners who have undergone formal theological education. Through this education they have learned to think critically about the present situation of the Church. They have become convinced for themselves of the need for the shift from maintenance to mission. And they are committed to being active agents in a missionary Church.

More generally, and perhaps more significantly, there is the growing number of parishioners who, without any formal formation of this kind, have come to see their participation in the parish in a new way. They no longer see themselves as passive and receptive. They want to have a voice and they desire to share the burden and the responsibility of caring for the future of their parish.

This corresponds closely to the thrust of *Christifideles Laici.* Since Vatican II, the Pope says, the Church has been coming to a new awareness of its missionary nature. But the call to work in the Lord's vineyard is addressed to everyone, not just priests and religious (paragraph 2). Part of the concern is pragmatic:

> ... at present the missionary concern is taking on such extensive and serious proportions for the Church that only a truly consolidated effort to assume responsibility by all members of the Church, both individuals and communities, can lead to the hope for a more fruitful response.' (paragraph 35)

But it is not just pragmatic. All the baptised, not just the ordained, share in the ministry of Christ (paragraph 34). Therefore all are responsible for mission. Indeed, as the document repeatedly implies, if parishioners are not actively involved in mission, the impression might well be created that mission is just something 'churchy' that priests engage in, rather than something concerned with daily life and its transformation in Christ.

Indeed the more it is reflected upon, the clearer it becomes that the participation of parishioners is crucial to the mission of the parish. For they share the same experience of life as their neighbours and as their own age group, young or old. They have the same concerns and difficulties. They speak the same language. Therefore, in a way that may not always be possible for the priest, they 'will be able to reach the hearts of their neighbours, friends and colleagues, opening them to a full sense of human existence' (CFL, paragraph 28).

But parishioners, no less than priests, require some form of re-education if mission is to become part of their consciousness. Simply saying it once or twice will make little impression in the face of attitudes that have been established for decades. People need the opportunity to reflect and to initiate themselves into the new mindset.

So, when we talk of priests and when we talk of parishioners, we find that the mindset of mission leads into the theme of collaboration. A shift from maintenance to mission is demanded if the parish is to be the kind of community where God's people can encounter Christ in their spiritual hunger and their spiritual quest. But this shift itself involves the further shift from a parish where the priest does everything to one where the burden of mission is shared by all.

A DIVINE MISSION

There is one further important dimension to the meaning of mission. It is only since Europeans discovered and conquered the Americas that 'mission' came to mean bringing the gospel to lands that had never heard of Christ.

But prior to the 1500s, mission was a word that belonged to the theology of the Trinity. On the one hand, it referred to the relationships between the three persons of the Trinity themselves.

On the other, it referred to the Father's 'sending' of the Son into the world and to their 'sending' of the Spirit to the disciples.

And it referred to the disciples themselves. 'As the Father has sent me, so I send you' (John 20: 21). Being sent, being missionary, is part of the essence of being a Christian, just as it is part of the reality of the Trinity. St Paul captured this when he said:

> But how are they to call on one in whom they have not believed? And how are they to believe in one of whom they have never heard? And how are they to hear without someone to proclaim him? And how are they to proclaim him unless they are sent? (Romans 10: 14-15)

Thus, while the parish will find today's missionary task daunting, engaging in that task is also a going back to the roots, a rediscovering of what Christianity is all about. To think in terms of mission is to think in terms of being at the service of God's own mission in the world, drawing people through the Spirit into the experience and knowledge of being sons and daughters in the Son, eternally and irrevocably loved.

Resources

Themes of this Chapter	**Resource Material in Vol II**
From maintenance to mission.	*From Maintenance to Mission,* sessions which take the parish group through what is involved in mission.
The mission of the parishioner.	*Called by Name,* session five.
Mission and the priest.	*The Priest and Parish Renewal,* sessions which take the parish team through what is involved in renewal.
Parish and mission.	*A Parish Renewal Mission,* an adaptation of the traditional parish mission.

CHAPTER 6

Outreach and Witness

The focus on mission is one that motivates and energises parish planning groups. There is great concern among committed parishioners over the fall-off in religious practice and the seeming loss of spirituality in contemporary culture. Their concern is strongest when they talk about young people, although it is not confined to young people. Talk of mission is, therefore, practical and real.

The concern is deeper still, for it reflects something that is at the heart of Christianity. In his encyclical letter on mission (*Redemptoris Missio,* paragraphs 5, 11), John Paul II reflects on the question, why mission? Mission arises, he says, from the conviction that in Christ, God has been revealed in a definitive fashion for all people.

This means that Christians cannot keep hidden the newness and the richness of knowing Christ. God's life within us demands to be made known and shared. To have the Spirit of Christ within us is a privilege, but the privilege is also an obligation. Each Christian must learn to say with St Paul, 'woe to me if I do not proclaim the gospel!' (1 Corinthians 9: 16).

Them or Us?

However, when people get down to teasing out the challenge of mission, very often it emerges that what seems like talk of a mission-centred Church proves to be talk of a church-centred mission. This is betrayed by the way in which questions are phrased. People ask, 'how can we bring them back?' The picture in many people's minds is one of filling the church again – 'putting bums on seats' as one person put it.

This kind of thinking often implies that the problem is them, not us. Sometimes it is linked to talk of 'where have the commandments gone?' and 'people have lost the sense of sin' and 'the young people just don't bother anymore'. There can even be an undertone of self-righteousness at times.

At the same time all this is understandable. Generally it is middle-aged people who are the first to become involved in parish renewal. They are naturally disappointed that the Church they grew up with and cherish dearly is on the decline. What would be more obvious to desire than that the church would once again be full and alive with the voices of young and old?

But if the matter is probed further, it emerges that it is not quite so simple. Ask these same people if they would like things to be once more what they were in, say, the 1950s, with churches full for Sundays and sodalities, confessions and missions, and the answer is a resounding and unequivocal 'No!'

People do not want to go back. For, when they reflect on it, they know that things were not perfect then. Churches were full, but much of it was an external religiosity only, or a response to a terribly tight social control. Then there was the rigorism, the fear, the lack of compassion, the intolerance of difference.

So the situation is far from black and white, it is far more complex. In talking about mission today, people may well start out from an attitude that suggests the problem to be them, not us. But reflection can lead them to the opposite conclusion, that they themselves, or at least the Church they grew up with, are part of the problem. They may even begin to feel angry about the Church. They may begin to understand why others might have stopped coming.

REASONS WHY PEOPLE HAVE LEFT

The complexity of the situation becomes even more evident when parishioners tease out the reasons why others have stopped coming. I say 'reasons' because it soon emerges that there is no one reason but rather a plurality of reasons.

Something of this is reflected in the vocabulary we use to designate those who no longer participate. We refer to them as 'lapsed' or 'alienated' or 'disaffected' or 'drifted' or 'marginalised' or 'inactive' or 'non-practising'. Words like 'inactive' are fairly neutral. Other words such as 'lapsed' suggest that it is their fault. Others such as 'alienated' carry a sense that the problem may be in the parish or the Church itself.

Hurt

Let us look, then, at the variety of reasons parishioners give as to why other parishioners have stopped coming to church. One reason is that a person, at some time in the past, underwent a negative experience. Perhaps it was something said by a priest in confession, or some unkindness or lack of attention. Whatever it was, it soured the person's experience of Church to the extent that he or she could no longer bear taking part.

Unworthy

Perhaps it was a sense of unworthiness. Many people feel unworthy because of their lifestyle – for instance, where a marriage has broken up and the person is in a second relationship. For many people this affects their relationship with God. They do not really think there is mercy available to them. Or else they sense that there is no mercy for them in the Church. Either way they feel excluded.

Church Teaching

Perhaps it was a disagreement with some Church teaching. This usually happens in the area of morality, particularly in issues to do with sexuality, marriage and procreation. In these issues the Church's position tends to be quite unbending, yet people conscientiously disagree and as a result feel themselves outside the fold.

Sometimes it is not so much that people disagree as that they find themselves unable, because of their circumstances, to observe the particular teaching. In that case they often feel a lack of compassion and understanding from a Church that seems to them more interested in rules and regulations than in people. Other times it is a misunderstanding of a particular teaching that leads to the sense of alienation.

Image of Church

The reason some people stop coming has to do with the image projected by the Church. Perhaps the person was offended by the power and wealth of the Church, or scandalised by its clericalism or sexism or authoritarianism. Or perhaps it was the image of the Church projected in some of the media which led to the alienation.

Or perhaps it was the perception that being a Catholic means being dependent and obedient rather than autonomous and responsible. Or that being a Catholic is something very 'churchy' rather than down to earth and integrated with real life. Much of this has to do with a failure on the part of the Church to communicate its message, and with a failure to use the modern media of communication to do so.

Impersonal Parish

Perhaps the reason was the impersonality of the parish in which the person lived. Often there is no welcome for new parishioners and often there is no contact made with those who are settled. Often there is no sense of hospitality and welcome at the church on Sunday, and not a priest in sight outside the church. With no sense of belonging to a living Christian community, no sense of the value of participating, many people just drift away.

Liturgy

Perhaps it had to do with the liturgy. Young people complain that the Mass is boring and, while others reply that young people should put more into Mass, I feel that what the young people say is valid. In some parishes relatively little preparation is put into the Sunday liturgy. Sometimes, scandalous as it sounds, the priest can look uninterested, just going through a routine. Rarely is there a homily that is addressed to the experience of young people.

But it is not just young people. Many others have found that Mass does not nourish them – they go away as spiritually hungry as when they arrived. Frequently there is a sense that people have to leave the great concerns of their daily lives in the porch, because they will not be 'taken up' onto the altar and into the Mass. The Mass seems to be about something else.

Others again have been alienated by sexism, most notably by the persisting exclusiveness of liturgical language. Others have found the same language to be far from their 'vernacular', too theological, too middle-class. Many of these people have gone in search of other ways of nourishing their spirituality.

Drifting

Other people just drift away, without making a conscious decision or thinking it through. Some people just do not bother, do not make the effort, are too lazy. They do not put in the work that is required if Christianity is to be taken seriously. So they never get around to praying or taking part in liturgy. Within no time at all following Christ has ceased to part of their consciousness.

Loss of Faith

For others again, it is that 'the bubble has burst'. Growing up in a secular, scientific, sceptical world, the beliefs and the magic of religion fall apart on them. Religion loses credibility. They feel they can get on fine without it. Meanwhile there are a lot of things in life in which to become absorbed. It is a world where the material has replaced the spiritual, where the distractions of life are many, where affluence blocks out God.

Some people experience a crisis of faith. Perhaps there were real doubts about God or about central doctrines of the Christian creed. The horrors of human suffering have left many unable to believe in a caring God. As a result, many are genuinely agnostic; while committed to human values they cannot see anything beyond the human.

Childish Faith

Perhaps the reason is a childish faith. There are very many people who have a third-level education but whose religious education has gone no further than primary school. It is understandable if they then reject religion as primitive and superstitious. Perhaps they never made the transition from a religion of conformity to a religion of conviction. Perhaps they never internalised their faith. Perhaps they rejected religion without ever having had a personal relationship with Jesus. If so, what they threw out was not real faith, but an impoverished version of faith.

Home

Perhaps the reason had to do with home. There may have been little or no religion in the home. Perhaps one or both of the parents never went to Mass or prayed. Or they may have come to feel negatively about the Church. The teachers in school might have done their best, as so often they do, to make up for what the children lacked at home, but it may not have been enough.

Poverty

Some people's leaving has to do with poverty. I have a picture in my mind of poor people in the past finding some comfort in religion amidst their hardships. Today this does not seem to be the case. Geographically, the areas of lowest practice are the areas of greatest hardship and adversity. Maybe people blame God for their situation. Maybe they think the parish is irrelevant to their needs.

MISSION TO WHOM?

The variety of reasons why people have ceased to be involved in the parish and the Church cannot be reduced to any one factor. Contemporary culture is a major cause, though it is only implicit in many of the factors just listed. The quality of a person's upbringing is also very significant, as are the circumstances of individual lives.

But equally, shortcomings in the Church itself and in the Church as reflected at parish level are a more significant factor than is often appreciated. Sometimes, of course, the problem is people's perception of religion rather than the reality itself. But that does not take away from the fact that the Church and the parish themselves are the focus of many of the difficulties.

Given the complexity of the factors involved it is, I think, fair to say that a person's ceasing to be involved, while regrettable, is not always a negative step. In the context of the person's own spiritual journey such a step may sometimes be an important stage in the emergence of a more personal and authentic faith.

This raises the question of the status in relation to Church and parish of those who have left. In the United States, where some dioceses have put a lot of energy into reaching out to the alienated, it has been reckoned that over 40% of those who have ceased to 'practise' are open to, if not desirous of, some form of re-engagement with the Church. Though no studies have been done in Ireland, it seems reasonable to presume that a similar, if not a higher, figure would be true of here.

But what kind of re-engagement? Some who have drifted away will drift back, perhaps on the occasion of the baptism or first communion of a child. Some will respond to a gesture like the 'Come Home for Christmas' message issued in the Dublin diocese some years ago. These are the people who are open at some stage to returning to the Church they left.

Others have no intention of returning. What they left, they left for a reason. They may find new channels or vehicles for their spiritual quest and hunger, but they will not go back to what they rejected. The only possibility of re-engagement in these cases is if there is something new offered by the Church itself.

We seem to have come full circle. We started out with people thinking that the problem is 'them not us'. Now it seems that, in many cases, the problem is us, not them. In light of the reasons why people have left, this appears to be irrefutable. So many – not all, but a striking number – of the reasons have to do with shortcomings on the side of the Church.

There come to mind Jesus' shocking words to the chief priests and the elders of the people: 'Truly I tell you, the tax collectors and the prostitutes are going into the kingdom of God ahead of you' (Matthew 21: 31). Maybe it is the case that those who no longer take part are more graced than we imagine and that those who are involved are themselves in need of conversion! There is obvious exaggeration in this, but there is a truth, though less obvious, as well.

The truth I am referring to is that mission is about those who are still involved no less than it is about those who have ceased participating. If we want to *reach out* to the alienated, we must also *reach in* to the involved. If we want to attract we have to be attractive.

MISSION AS WITNESS

We have a tendency to head straight into action, even though there might not be a lot to offer to those who have lost contact with the parish. There can be a tendency to presume that it is all just a matter of going out there and 'bringing them back'. A little more reflection on why people have drifted away dispels that presumption. There is much to be sorted out in the parish itself before it thinks of reaching out. Before the question of outreach there is the question of *witness*.

Looking at Ourselves

The call to mission, therefore, is a call to look at ourselves. The reasons why people have left are saying something about ourselves, either ourselves as a parish or ourselves as a Church. We need to acknowledge that:

- People have been hurt.

- There has been a lack of compassion, and a judgmental and legalistic attitude.

- We have suffered from authoritarianism, sexism, clericalism.

- Liturgies have been off-putting and alienating.

- Parishes have been impersonal and unwelcoming.

- Communications have left much to be desired.

- People have found their spiritual hunger unfulfilled in the parish.

- The image of Christianity projected has often been less than attractive.

This is not to say that everything is dismal, or that all the fault for people's disenchantment with religion lies with the Church and the parish. It is simply to say that the first step is *to learn from the reasons for people's leaving,* because these reasons have a considerable amount to teach the Church about itself.

In particular, they strongly suggest the need for Church and parish to get back to their own roots, to rediscover what being a Christian community is all about. Here we can recall what was said in chapter three about what the parish might become, as well as the way that this was linked to the description of the early Christian community in the Acts of the Apostles.

In his writings on discipleship, Eamon Bredin spells out some of what is meant here by getting back to the roots (cf. *The Furrow*, July 1981, pp 415-427). He speaks about what he calls the problem of familiarity. When we become too familiar with something or someone, we begin to take things for granted. The original spark and excitement disappear. Complacency sets in.

So with Christ. Where we are meant to be disturbed out of our own world and challenged to enter his world, we can end up doing the opposite. We can settle him down in a corner of our world, where he will not cause any disturbance. As Bredin puts it, we 'domesticate' Christ. As a result we end up in a position where we 'prefer coma to challenge'.

The opposite of familiarity is discipleship. Though we tend to reserve this word for the twelve apostles, in fact it is meant for all of us. Discipleship, or following Christ, suggests adventure. It suggests the excitement of being called and responding, of feeling that here there is 'something to live for, great enough to die for'. It suggests that responding to Christ has become the inspiration of a person's life.

The point is this: which better captures the tone and texture of our parish communities – the 'coma' of familiarity or the spark of discipleship? The implications are clear. Those who are still involved need themselves to undergo some form of re-evangelisation, so as to rediscover what it really means to be a Christian. Many have drifted away without any conscious decision but something similar is true of many who have stayed on. We all need to think through just what we believe in.

Maybe, if this issue is highlighted, we will discover that a number of those who still take part are not really interested. But that is the risk. The first challenge of mission is to build the people into a community of disciples.

Renewal is Mission; Mission is Renewal

This may sound more like 'parish renewal' than 'mission', and well it might. It tells us, on the one hand, that parish renewal is not fully understood until it is seen in the context of mission and in its implications for mission. On the other hand it tells us that mission is only properly grasped when it is based in the renewal of the parish. This I would interpret to be the meaning of the following passage from John Paul II:

> Communion and mission are profoundly connected with each other, they interpenetrate and mutually imply each other, to the point that communion represents both the source and the fruit of mission: communion gives rise to mission and mission is accomplished in communion. (CFL, paragraph 32)

To renew the sense of discipleship at the heart of parish community; this is missionary or evangelising activity. As mission, it is also reaching out indirectly to others who have lost contact with parish. It is reaching out in the form of witness.

Just as many have been put off by the image projected by the Church – the image of Christianity, the image of God – so many may be attracted by a more authentic image. As was stressed by the Pope in *Redemptoris Missio,* the witness of Christian living is 'the first and irreplaceable form of mission' (paragraph 42).

This brings us back again to the Acts of the Apostles. As it describes a Christian community afire with the Spirit, it also says: 'Awe came upon everyone, because many wonders and signs were being done by the apostles...And day by day the Lord added to their number those who were being saved' (Acts 2: 43, 47).

Then as now, Christian community was attractive. The witness was itself mission, itself a form of reaching out. And when Christians go on to reach out more directly to others, that itself is a form of community-building, as more people come to experience the reach of God's loving embrace.

So, mission begins with the parish striving to be what it might become – a place of hospitality (especially for those who have any reason to doubt their welcome); a community imbued with a deep sense of being loved by God; where the experience of liturgy is full of vitality; where people are encouraged in their giftedness and in a sense of responsibility for each other. Where this is happening, so much of mission is *already* being accomplished. The parish community is being re-evangelised and is becoming an attractive witness for others.

MISSION AS OUTREACH

In this way renewal and mission come together. Mission as witness shades into mission as outreach. I now wish to describe how a parish, already concerned for the renewal of those still involved, can reach out to others. What I have in mind is not so much the strategies that might be adopted, but the *disposition* with which the outreach is undertaken.

The 'Practising Catholic'

I begin by reflecting on what we understand by the term a 'practising Catholic'. I recall some time ago a discussion where one parishioner took exception to the phrase. He said he did not go to Mass every Sunday but did go fairly often, yet he felt defined as 'non-practising' because he did not go each week. So where do we draw the line? What constitutes a practising Catholic?

When we think about it, we can see that 'practice' involves much more besides going to Mass. Of course a link is missing if some Christians are not part of the community's ritual. Nevertheless, 'practising' involves a number of elements, such as:

- A personal prayer life of ongoing communication between the individual and the Lord.
- Faith seeking understanding and an ever-deepening appreciation of what is believed.
- Relationships with others, a commitment to quality of relationship and to putting Christianity into 'practice' in relationships with others.
- A sense of responsibility to the community and a willingness to play one's part.
- A sense of justice and a deep concern for right relationships throughout society.

Compare this to what John Paul II says about the multifaceted nature of following Christ. Each baptised person follows Christ

> ... in embracing the Beatitudes, in listening and meditating on the Word of God, in conscious and active participation in the liturgical and sacramental life of the Church, in personal prayer, in family or in community, in the hunger and thirst

> for justice, in the practice of the commandment of love in all circumstances of life and service to the brethren, especially the least, the poor and the suffering. (CFL, paragraph 16)

This brings to mind what the Old Testament prophets insisted on so frequently, that ritual without the serious practice of justice is a lie (e.g. Isaiah 58; Jeremiah 22: 16; Amos 5: 21-24). The same concern is close to the heart of Jesus. He says that it is not those who say 'Lord, Lord' who will enter the kingdom, but those who do the will of God (Matthew 7: 21). In a more famous passage whose refrain is, 'insofar as you did it to one of these, you did it to me' (Matthew 25: 31-46), he says that the test of faith is in how we live.

Who, then, is a practising Catholic? Most of us would admit to being imperfect in some aspect. One person goes to Mass and prays regularly, but puts little or nothing into relationships with others, or cares little about the poor. Another has a personal prayer life but no commitment to the community. Another is passionate about justice in society but never goes to Mass and has no relationship with God. Can we say that one 'practises' better than the others?

Prayer, fasting and almsgiving are regarded as 'pillars' of our religion (cf. Matthew 6: 1-18). Yet young people, frequently spoken of as the ones who do not practise their religion, score highly on these. They are more enthusiastic than most about alternative forms of prayer. They are the ones who participate in twenty-four hour fasts. They give alms by collecting money for so many causes. It is to be lamented if they do not appreciate the communal celebration of the Eucharist, but it seems unfair to dismiss them as not 'practising' on that account.

A Positive Disposition

Seen from this angle, the practice rate in the parish is probably much higher than the rate of Mass attendance! The spirit of mission is to acknowledge this and to find ways of affirming it. While we are inclined to bemoan the absence of many from the Eucharistic celebration, it may be much more life-giving to recognise and respond to the *spirituality* that is still alive in the way the 'non-practising' live their lives.

Somebody once said that mission is not so much about bringing God to people who do not have God, but rather a matter of affirming the God already present in people's hearts and lives. This may be part of what is meant by the doctrine of the 'mystical body' of Christ. 'Church' is happening, not just in the visible presence of many on Sunday, but also in less visible ways, as yet implicit and waiting to be acknowledged.

So we can speak of a shift of attitude, from one of judging to one of understanding, from trying to 'bring them back' to trying to appreciate what it was that led to this situation. On the basis of this, the first point is that outreach should be conducted in a spirit of affirmation. It is the spirit that says that today 'too often people do not know what they carry inside, in the deepest recesses of their soul, in their heart' (CFL, paragraph 34).

The second point, really an elaboration of this, is that outreach is about listening to and being with people. There are many among those whom we are trying to reach who have been hurt by the Church, or who have felt excluded in their disagreement or nonconformity with Church teaching. With these people mission begins, not by speaking, but by listening and giving a voice.

Others whom we are trying to reach are out of contact for reasons to do with their poverty or brokenness or suffering or hardship. In these cases mission means simply being with, accompanying. It offers, not solutions, but solidarity, a presence in which Christ himself is present.

In this spirit, mission is about initiating a relationship and initiating a process. It is not a matter of 'we'll listen or be with *in order that* thereby they will return to the fold'. Rather it is a matter of listening and being with because God is in this place and in this person. What happens next will be the fruit of the process.

If this is the disposition, new possibilities will suggest themselves. They will include alternative ways of expressing and nourishing the spiritual hunger in people. They will include alternative forms of prayer and ritual. They will include creative forms of adult religious education that can overcome the misapprehensions that exist about what it is to be a Christian. Making contact is not easy, but the first step is having the right disposition.

In all this, parishioners rather than priests may be the key, for the reason stated at the end of the last chapter. It is they who are neighbours and friends of those to whom outreach is directed, and who are therefore in the best position to communicate the gospel in a credible and fruitful way. Again the evidence from the United States is instructive; in reaching out to the 'alienated', the most significant factor is the witness of neighbours and friends.

Conclusion to Part One

In this first part of the book I have been describing a new way of thinking about the parish. This new way begins in an attitude of hope, trusting that God continues to work amongst us. It sees both hope and challenge in the persistence of the spiritual. It envisages a parish where this spirituality is expressed and fulfilled. It takes on a mindset of mission, committed to a redirection of time and energy. It engages in this redirection in a positive disposition of affirmation, listening and companionship.

In part two, our attention shifts to how this new way of thinking, this new mindset, this new vision, this new disposition, is to become a reality. I will be proposing that the key lies in priests and parishioners sharing responsibility for the future of the parish - in a spirit of hope, taking responsibility together for their future as God's people.

Resources

Themes of this Chapter	Resource Material in Vol II
Reasons why people have left.	*From Maintenance to Mission*, session two.
	Called by Name, session five, on the obstacles to people experiencing God in their lives.
Both outreach and witness.	*From Maintenance to Mission*, session three, on guiding principles for action.
The practising Catholic.	*Called by Name*, session four.
Priorities for mission.	*Choosing a Model of Operating*, session six.

In addition, *Spirituality for Today* is a set of sessions designed in particular for people who are no longer involved in the parish but who are still open to the spiritual.

PART II

The way forward – sharing responsibility

CHAPTER 7

Christianity *is* collaboration

We come now to the core idea of parish renewal. It goes by different names. Some call it 'lay involvement'; others call it 'collaboration'; others 'shared responsibility'; others again 'partnership'. None of the terms are perfect, least of all those using the word 'lay' (as we shall see in the next chapter).

The core idea itself is about parishioners sharing responsibility for the care and the future of their parish – as opposed to the priest or priests carrying this burden on their own, as if it were 'the priest's job'. Nor is collaboration the same as 'delegation' or 'consultation', for these terms still presume that renewal is ultimately the priest's job.

I have already quoted Cardinal Tomás Ó Fiaich's reference to the laity as the 'sleeping giant' in the church. Parish renewal is about the awakening of that giant. The word 'giant' does not refer to numbers only but to potential – to energy, to resourcefulness, to commitment, to hope. The parishioners who are available to give themselves to the care of their parishes are the hope of the Church. This cannot be overstated. To fail to see this is to be hopeless.

This idea of shared responsibility has already come up a number of times in the first part of this volume. There we saw that part of the challenge of mission is the challenge to priests and parishioners to *share responsibility* for mission. This second part of the volume focuses in on that theme.

Something that is Right

Subsequent chapters will tease out the dynamics of shared responsibility, as well as the underlying theology of laity, ministry and priesthood. In this chapter I want to set out the context in which the subsequent discussion can be properly appreciated. This context concerns the sense in which shared responsibility lies at the very heart of Christian faith.

I recall being involved towards the end of the 1970s in the preparation programme for the ministers of the Eucharist then being introduced in the Dublin diocese. There was a debate at the time as to what precisely was the rationale for their introduction. Was it to maintain previous levels of service in the context of a declining number of priests? Or was it something that was desirable in its own right, an expression of the ministry of the people of the parish themselves?

If it was the former then, the argument could continue, were the number of priests to increase again, there would no longer be any need for the supplementing. Decades later we can smile as we recall this debate, for now it is so obviously redundant. Ministry is not confined to the ordained and we cherish this and other comparable enrichments of parish life.

But the debate continues in a much more important way. Now it revolves around, not ministers of the Eucharist, but what we call collaborative ministry or collaborative leadership, meaning the involvement of parishioners with priests in a shared responsibility for the *whole* of parish life.

In some places this takes the form of a parish council. Elsewhere something looser has emerged, variously called a parish planning group or a parish core group or a parish forum. Here, the focus is on the group growing into a vision of parish and an ethos of collaboration, with the emphasis on the process rather than the structure, on the pastoral rather than the administrative.

But the same question arises as arose in the 1970s. Is this happening because there are less and less priests, because we need more hands on deck? Or is it because this is something that is right in itself, something that should be happening whatever the circumstances? If the so-called 'crisis of vocations' were to resolve itself in the morning, would the movement towards shared responsibility for the parish evaporate?

In the same way that we now look back with a smile at the debate surrounding the introduction of ministers of the Eucharist, so in decades to come we will look back on the current debate. Pragmatic needs may have facilitated the introduction of collaboration, but collaboration does not rest on pragmatic motives, any more than does the presence of ministers of the Eucharist.

Parishioners sharing responsibility for the care and the future of their parishes is a theological insight and a theological truth. The circumstances of the current situation have occasioned this sharing, but it transcends the circumstances. It is simply something that is right.

Collaboration in leadership is not an emergency procedure. It is not a stop-gap measure or a last-ditch effort. It is not a technique, a means to an end. Its justification is not that it is the most effective way of dealing with the situation. It exists, not because it works, or because it might work, but because it is right. It pertains to the essence of what it is to be a Christian.

THE WORD OF GOD

Sharing the Burden

I wish to present, firstly, some insights from scripture which give depth to the contemporary experience of collaboration. The first insight comes from the Old Testament, from the Book of Numbers. The people are in the desert and they are complaining about their misfortunes. Moses hears their weeping, the Lord is becoming angry, and Moses is displeased. His displeasure is expressed as a cry about the situation in which he finds himself. He speaks to the Lord:

> Why have you treated your servant so badly? Why have I not found favour in your sight, that you lay the burden of all this people on me? Did I conceive all this people? Did I give birth to them, that you should say to me, 'Carry them in your bosom, as a nurse carries a sucking child,' to the land that you promised on oath to their ancestors? Where am I to get meat to give to all this people? For they come weeping to me and say, 'Give us meat to eat!' I am not able to carry all these people alone, for they are too heavy for me. If this is the way you are going to treat me, put me to death at once – if I have found favour in your sight – and do not let me see my misery. (Numbers 11: 11-15; cf. Exodus 18: 13-25)

The Lord responds readily. Seventy of those 'whom you know to be the elders of the people' are gathered. The Lord takes some of the spirit that is on Moses and puts it on them – 'and they shall bear the burden of the people along with you, so that you will not bear it all by yourself'.

It is undoubtedly pragmatic, a matter of dealing with a situation. The incident tells us of a pragmatism that is at the heart of salvation. But it is not pragmatism in the crude political sense of doing whatever needs to be done in order to survive. It is pragmatism in the sense of responding to need. The needs of God's people are at the centre of salvation history. Responding to those needs is the priority. The spiritual hunger is what matters.

This incident contains the further insight that collaboration is not about power. Priests frequently speak about collaboration in these terms, partly due to their being brought up in too canonical a view of leadership. They fear a loss of power. The reasons for this vary. Some fear that, because they have been entrusted with the responsibility for the parish, any loss of control may put the well-being of the parish at risk. The fear is genuine, if misguided. Others simply do not like the prospect of not being in control.

The insight is that collaboration is not primarily about sharing power (at least in the crude conception of what 'power' means), but about sharing a burden. Moses was not worried about a diminution of his power base. He just could not cope on his own with the demands of leadership. This is a reflection of the common and deep human instinct for help. To acknowledge the need for help and the desirability of help is an expression of hope, not of despair. It expresses our sense that together we may have the resources that are needed.

Collaboration is not about power, it is about care. It asks the question; how are these people to be cared for? It shifts the question from 'how am I to do all this?' to 'how are we together going to care for God's people?' This should resonate loudly with our experience today – the number of priests decreasing, the demands of mission increasing. For us, and for priests specifically, it shifts the question from 'how am *I* going to manage?' to 'how are *we* going to respond?'

Vocations in Plenty

The experience of Moses has echoes in the gospels. The first of these echoes is in chapter ten of Luke's gospel, where the number seventy recurs. Jesus had already chosen the twelve ('whom he also named apostles', Luke 6: 13):

> After this the Lord appointed seventy others and sent them on ahead of him in pairs to every town and place where he

> himself intended to go. He said to them, 'The harvest is plentiful, but the labourers are few; therefore ask the Lord of the harvest to send out labourers into his harvest... (Luke 10: 1-2)

The way in which this text is generally used has the effect of obscuring the theme of collaboration which it shares with the text from Numbers. The text is almost always used to speak about 'vocations', meaning vocations to the priesthood and the religious life. This is hard to defend today. I know of nothing about this text which requires or even indicates this interpretation. If anything it should be the opposite. The twelve have already been called; this is about a further dimension of ministry!

One exception to the common interpretation comes from John Paul II (CFL, paragraph 2). He quotes from the Vatican II document on the laity, regarding the mission of all God's people, that the Lord 'sends them into every town and place where he himself is to come'. The text refers explicitly to the above passage from Luke. Here at least, the 'labourers' are understood to be, not priests, but parishioners.

What then does Jesus want us to ask of 'the Lord of the harvest'? Does he ask us to pray for vocations to the priesthood? Again, the text itself contains nothing about this. Yet we continue to pray for vocations to the priesthood. The response is poor. Does this mean that what Jesus asks us to pray for will not be given? That is hardly likely. Perhaps, then, we are asking in the wrong place. Perhaps we should look to the 'vocations' that are there, namely, the substantial number of lay people who are ready to work, as *Christifideles Laici* puts it, in 'the Lord's vineyard'.

And the number is substantial. Large numbers of parishioners are deeply committed to their parishes and anxious to put their energy into the mission of the parish. Many of them have put the time into becoming qualified in theology, in pastoral ministry, in catechetics, in prayer ministry. I find myself asking; is there a crisis in vocations or is there a crisis in *the way we see vocations*? Is it that Jesus' prayer is being answered, but that we are looking in the wrong places? Is it that the 'vocations' are there, but that we cannot see it?

There is Enough

The second echo in the gospels of Moses' experience is to be found in the story of the feeding of the five thousand (Mark 6:

30-44). We heard the cry of Moses, 'Where am I to get meat to give to all this people?' In the feeding of the five thousand his cry is echoed by the disciples asking Jesus; 'Are we to go and buy two hundred denarii worth of bread, and give it to them to eat?' It is the same cry in both cases; how are we to care for so many? In both, the burden seems so great, the resources seem so few.

Jesus says to his disciples; 'How many loaves have you? Go and see.' They are to look again. As the story unfolds they learn that there is enough. It is this sense that there is enough, communicated by the Lord, that draws Moses back from misery and the disciples back from helplessness. There is no need, as the disciples first thought, to go off somewhere else to obtain what it needed. What is needed is here among us. It is a matter of our being able to see it. This corresponds to what I said earlier; God's purposes *are* being achieved, our task is to discern how and where.

A priest I worked with once used to say now and then about different people who were involved in the parish, 'you could ordain them in the morning'. It is the same point; there is enough. Among God's people in the parish there are extraordinary depths of faith. There are unexplored reserves of commitment and energy. There are unacknowledged gifts for leadership in a whole range of parish activities.

Other priests, however, will say that they have looked for these people and that they could not find them. They may add that people are so busy with other commitments, they do not have the time for this work of parish renewal (there will be some further discussion of these difficulties in the next chapter). Sometimes these comments are genuine and sometimes they are more disingenuous.

The comments are realistic in that it takes work to identify people for and initiate them into collaboration. It is, after all, a radically new way of going about things, one that parishioners are not used to, any more than priests. And, of course, the process has to be attuned to the time commitments people are actually able to make, which will vary from person to person.

On the disingenuous side, priests themselves can be lacking in conviction about the truth of collaboration. If they are not convinced or not interested, they are not going to see or find what is there. They will be looking in the wrong places; they will be looking in the wrong way. They may even be looking in the hope of not finding anything!

But the evidence is there from the majority of parishes. There is enough. The issue, as with the disciples, is our capacity to see. Indeed, just as their experience concludes with twelve baskets being filled with the leftovers, so in our case it is not just that there is enough or barely enough. There is more than enough.

The fact is that we are in a time of grace and that this is the grace for our times. God's purposes are being achieved and in parishes this is taking the form of more and more parishioners becoming available to share the responsibility for the care and the future of their Christian communities.

The Body of Christ

I said that collaboration is a radically new way of going about things. But, as with other new departures in today's Church, it is also very old. There are passages in the letters of St Paul which affirm that this spirit of collaboration was at the heart of the earliest efforts to build Christian community.

Writing to the Ephesians, Paul encourages them to maintain amongst themselves the unity of 'the one body' of Christ. In this unity,

> ...each of us was given grace according to the measure of Christ's gift... The gifts he gave were that some would be apostles, some prophets, some evangelists, some pastors and teachers, to equip the saints for the work of ministry, for building up the body of Christ... (Ephesians 4: 7, 11)

Writing to the Romans, Paul is again encouraging the life of discipleship and again he speaks of the one body. We who are many are one body in Christ, but not all members have the same function. 'We have gifts that differ according to the grace given to us' – gifts of prophecy, ministering, teaching, exhortation, generous giving, diligent leadership, cheerful compassion (Romans 12: 4-8).

The most extensive passage is addressed to the Corinthians (1 Corinthians 12). Again Paul speaks of the variety of gifts, all given for the common good, for the building up of the Christian community. The gifts he mentions in this case are wisdom, knowledge, faith, healing, the working of miracles, prophecy, the discernment of spirits, tongues and the interpretation of tongues. At the end of the chapter he goes on to mention apostles, teachers, those who do deeds of power, forms of assistance and forms of leadership.

But in between he speaks again of the one body, this time elaborating at some length on the analogy of the human body. We are all members of the same body, each part needing the others - if anything, the parts that seem to be weaker being the ones that are indispensable. The oneness is such that 'If one member suffers, all suffer together with it; if one member is honoured, all rejoice together with it' (12: 26).

In what Paul says to each of these three communities, the pattern is identical. There is a wide range of 'ministries' corresponding to a wide range of giftedness. And it is spread right across the community, not by any means confined to those in leadership positions. The gifts include, not just the 'official' ones such as teaching, but also very 'ordinary' ones such as 'cheerful compassion'. As gifts are exercised they form a harmony, all working together ('collaborating') for the building up of the community. In this way all the baptised really share the responsibility for the care of the body.

Because of the common pattern, what Paul says transcends the circumstances of any individual community, so as to stand as a truth about Christian community as such. It is the truth of collaboration. Each baptised person is gifted. The giftedness of each is itself a gift for the sake of all, for what Paul calls the 'upbuilding' of the community, since all are united as are the members of a human body.

It is this giftedness and collaboration that are at the heart of Christian community. We could even say that Christian community *is* a process of giftedness being affirmed and its being exercised in a collaborative spirit for the building up of the unity of the body of Christ.

The last phrase is vital. We are not talking here of any form of community, but rather of the distinctive form of Christian community, one which has no parallel. What the title 'the Body of Christ' indicates is that the spirit of collaboration at the heart of Christian community is something that reaches into God, just as the head and the body of each human person reach into each other. Collaboration, in other words, is telling us something about God.

SALVATION AS COLLABORATION

The deeper truth is that collaboration or shared responsibility is intrinsic to God's design or plan of salvation. All the history of salvation is a story of God and humankind working together, sharing responsibility for the future of creation.

From the beginning of the Bible there is dialogue. There is a two-way process between God and ourselves. There is God's invitation into Covenant relationship; there is our response. Just as there can be no response unless there is an invitation, so the invitation remains incomplete without the response. God and humanity are bound together in relationship, each needing the other if salvation is to be realised.

The relationship reaches its pinnacle in the Incarnation. Jesus, true God and truly one of us, is the perfect togetherness of God and humanity. The history of working together, of sharing responsibility, attains its perfect realisation in this moment. All subsequent history will follow the same pattern. This is what St Paul is articulating. As Christians collaborate through the mutual sharing of their giftedness, they strive towards the perfect realisation of unity in the body of Christ. The Incarnation becomes a present reality.

In the history of salvation, therefore, God's way or God's design is to involve us and to trust us. Another approach might well have been more efficient. God might well have decided that it would be quicker and easier if we were not involved, if everything were done by God. As it is, God has chosen the messier way! In creating human freedom God has let go the controls, has allowed the process of salvation to be co-determined by us, has entered into collaboration.

All of this is affirmed in our theology of grace. In choosing to save us, God did not choose to save us without our own cooperation. Salvation begins and ends in God's grace, but it involves both grace and freedom. Failures to get this balance right account for most of the great difficulties in the history of theology.

On one side there have been the misapprehensions which think that everything is done by God, so that there is essentially no sharing of responsibility. On the other side have been the misapprehensions which think that we can get on quite well unaided by God's grace.

A Spirituality

God's design is that history would be a process where God and humankind learn how to be together, how to collaborate, how to share responsibility. If this is so, then this is also to be the pattern of all Christian existence. All of Christian life and all of the life of the Christian community should be permeated by the spirit of collaboration that lies at the heart of salvation history itself.

Christian life should be a learning of what it means to affirm each other's giftedness, what it means to trust, what it means to work together as a single body. Most of all, it should be a learning of what it means to work in collaboration with God's grace. Another way of saying this is to say that collaboration is a *spirituality*.

> Collaborative ministry draws deeply upon faith in the Trinity. It is not simply a way of re-organising work or structures. It is a way of expressing in our life together what God asks of us and calls us to be. It is therefore a spirituality in it-

> self. Collaboration searches us, scrutinises our hearts and minds in the light of the Gospel and Trinitarian faith. It asks us to reflect what God is like in the ways we live and work together.' (*The Sign We Give*, page 35)

The obvious question is: have we misrepresented this spirit? Or have we failed to realise that this *is* the spirit of Christianity? It seems to have been well understood by St Paul but thereafter it would seem to have got lost. Subsequent history saw the disappearance of the variety of gifts and ministries reflected in Paul's writings – or, rather, the collapsing of these into the one ministry of the ordained. From then on, 'church' became synonymous with 'hierarchy' and 'clergy'. To this extent, the history of the church has not been a history of sharing responsibility.

This is what we have inherited from the past. We have a spirit of 'leave it to Father'. Priests have an attitude of 'it's easier and quicker if I do it'. We are used to being recipients of services. All this means, of course, that a great many things have been done with great efficiency, as is regularly the case when doing something oneself is preferred to doing it together. But in the process something has been missed, something that is the very spirit of what we believe.

The challenge of collaboration, thus, is not about a last resort when our backs are pinned to the wall. It is the challenge of recovering a dimension of salvation history that has been neglected. It is the challenge of getting back to our roots, back to the original spirit of what Christianity is all about. Any onus of proof there may be does not rest on those who would propose shared responsibility in the parish. It rests on those who would oppose it.

Resources

Themes of this Chapter	**Resource Material in Vol II**
Theology of collaboration.	*The Core Group and Parish Renewal*, sessions three and four.
Collaboration in the core group.	*Choosing a Model of Operating*, on a way of operating that reflects the spirit of collaboration.
	Working Well as a Group, particularly session five.

CHAPTER 8

All are called

What I have been saying about the themes of mission and collaboration implies a fundamental review of how we understand the parish. It asks for this review on the part of both priests and parishioners. Often there is resistance to this review, or else a failure to appreciate its significance.

I will be going into the reasons for this, but one of the reasons is simply people's familiarity with the Church and the parish as they have been. This familiarity makes it hard to envisage anything different. This applies, not just to people's understanding of parish, but also to their understanding of their own place or role within the parish. In other words, for anybody, priest or parishioner, to review their understanding of parish is also to review *their understanding of themselves* in the parish.

This chapter and the next are concerned with the self-understanding of parishioners, with what it means to be a parishioner in this context of the changing face of the parish. This is what is sometimes referred to as the theology of the 'laity'. As we proceed it will become clear that shared responsibility and collaboration are an intrinsic dimension of what it means to be a parishioner today.

'LAITY'

From the outset we are confronted with a problem of language. Up to now I have often used the word 'parishioner' instead of 'laity'. The connotations of the latter term render it, I suspect, one that is becoming less and less serviceable in thinking and talking about the parish.

A Negative Term

Something of this problem is acknowledged by John Paul II. He speaks of 'the need for a definition of the lay faithful's vocation and mission in positive terms', referring in this context to 'previous interpretations which were predominantly negative' (CFL, paragraph 9).

The idea here is that the word 'laity' defines people by what they are not. To be a lay person in the Church means not to be ordained. This is related to the identification of 'Church' with clergy and hierarchy that began to happen from early on in the history of Christianity. From this identification there developed the sense that to be a lay person meant to be 'on the outside looking in'.

Unqualified

The term has other unfortunate connotations as well. In ordinary usage to be a 'lay person' means to be unqualified and not competent to comment. Thus, while I am an ordained priest I am a lay person when it comes to medicine or to law. I am an amateur who needs to consult the expertise of the professionals.

Something of this transfers over into Church usage. Just as in medicine there are doctors and lay people, so in the Church to be a lay person has carried some sense of not being an expert, of being unqualified to comment. Lay people's competence has been seen to lie in secular affairs. When it comes to the things of God they must refer to and defer to the priests.

As an example of this, take what the French theologian Yves Congar said in the 1950s about lay people and theology. The laity can 'never handle theology like priests, they have never quite the same contact with the Church's tradition... Theology properly so called is pre-eminently a clerical, priestly learning' (*Lay People in the Church,* London, Chapman, 1985, page 310).

This view may have made sense in the context in which it was proposed, with theology seen as intimately related to the liturgical ministry of the priest. But it leaves a legacy nonetheless, a sense of lay people trespassing on what is not their proper field of activity.

Two-Tier Spirituality

Again, the distinction between clergy and laity carries within it some element of a two-tier spirituality. Up until recently (at least), Church documents have repeatedly affirmed that virginity is a higher state of life than marriage. This goes far back into the

Church's history. It expresses a sense from early on that to be a 'complete' Christian demands the renunciation of everything, including marriage. There simply would not be time for anything else.

This in turn implies that lay people, those not in religious life or ordained, are in a kind of second division. It is rather like the honours and pass courses in public examinations. The perception persists that there are degrees of holiness and that some degrees of holiness are not accessible without religious vows or ordination.

Passivity

Finally, to be a lay person in the parish implies passivity. The priest in the pulpit preaches and the people listen. This symbolises a relationship which most people can recognise. It is a one-way relationship and a one-way communication. The priest is the active one, at the centre, in control. The people are on the receiving end – called, as the saying goes, to 'pray, pay and obey'.

All this, I would emphasise, does not represent everybody's experience today, for things are changing. But it represents much of what has been and which still is the case in a great many places. More importantly, it represents what still is in a great many minds, clerical and lay.

But the only point I wish to take from this for now is that perhaps we need another word. Because of the connotations that have accrued to the word 'laity', the word may be unable to bear the weight of meaning which is being attached to it today. For today's theology is very much about somebody who is an insider, who is qualified, who is on the same spiritual level as everybody else, and who is an active agent in the life of the parish.

ALL ARE RESPONSIBLE

The first point to be made in presenting a more positive approach is that it is baptism, not holy orders, which is fundamental in the church. Perhaps the clearest statement of this came in the Vatican Council's document on the Church (*Lumen Gentium*). In the formulation of that document, a deliberate decision was made to put the chapter on 'The People of God' before the chapter on 'The Church is hierarchical'.

Communion

The significance of this is considerable. Before there is any distinction between 'clergy' and 'laity', all God's people share the same essential dignity by virtue of their common baptism. All are fundamentally equal. One way in which contemporary theology acknowledges this is in insisting that, while the Church is hierarchical, it is *fundamentally* a community or communion of those who are baptised .

> Communion is the nature of the church and the source of the relationships between all the baptised... [Hierarchy is] a structure for ordering and unifying relationships, a service to communion... We see hierarchy in the context of communion. (*The Sign we Give*, pages 20-22)

It is interesting here to reflect on the derivation of the word 'lay'. It comes from the Greek word *laos* which means people – the *laos* is the people. Thus, we would expect, the opposite would be 'not the people' – in other words, the foreigner, the stranger, the alien.

And this used to be the case. But in the early Church something else happened. As the Church became more clericalised, the gap between clergy and laity widened. The opposite of *laos,* the laity, the people, came to be the clergy, the hierarchy, those in official positions.

Again, the significance of this is considerable. When the opposite of the people is 'not the people', then the people are the insiders. But when the opposite is the clergy, then the clergy are the insiders, and the people, the laity, are the 'outsiders looking in'. Holy orders, not baptism, becomes primary.

This is what is changing today and it is what is reflected in the seemingly unimportant matter of the sequence of chapters in Vatican II's *Lumen Gentium.* Baptism is primary, all are equally the people of God. The fundamental truth is that all are insiders, all belong.

Baptism

I will elaborate on this briefly by reflecting on the meaning of being baptised, of being confirmed and of participating in the Eucharist – the three moments in the sacramental 'initiation' of the Christian.

Baptism today means 'welcome'. Formerly, the emphasis was

on original sin being wiped off the individual soul. Today we have rediscovered the communal dimension of the sacrament whereby the community welcomes this new person into its midst. As it does, it incarnates God's own welcome.

> With Baptism we become children of God in his only-begotten Son, Jesus Christ. Rising from the waters of the Baptismal font, every Christian hears again the voice that was once heard on the banks of the Jordan River: 'You are my beloved Son; with you I am well pleased (CFL, paragraph 11).

Baptism is the basic experience of being a Christian, for it is the experience of being told by God that 'you are my beloved'. To be a Christian is to be loved, to be loved by the Creator of the universe, to be loved unreservedly and eternally.

If this is what it means to *be* a Christian, then to *become* a Christian is to come to know this and appreciate it and live from it - to discover, as Jean Vanier put it, that we are lovable and able to love. This is the kind of thing that is meant to be happening within the Christian community.

Confirmation

Confirmation originally went with baptism, as a second moment in the sacrament, and still does when it is an adult who is being baptised. What confirmation means (and it is clearer in the adult ceremony than in the case of eleven- and twelve-year olds) is that being a Christian takes each of us beyond ourselves.

Baptism tells us that we are loved eternally in the depths of our being. But, while we are meant to enjoy this knowledge, it is not a cause for sitting back and doing nothing further. Rather, it puts us in contact with others who are similarly blessed. It inspires us towards affirming others in the same knowledge. This is what confirmation is about.

As Enda Lyons puts it in his *Partnership in Parish* (page 25), in being confirmed 'a person is commissioned to take on responsibility for the Church's task'. In baptism a person discovers the giftedness of being loved and lovable. In confirmation it is proclaimed that this giftedness is given for the common good, for the building up of the Christian community – what we heard St Paul speaking of in the last chapter.

If baptism is the gift, confirmation is the task. In being confirmed the Christian becomes co-responsible for the life of the community. We are all responsible for all, all responsible for the building up of a communion where all discover that they are lovable and able to love.

Eucharist

Eucharist might be described as the continuing sacramental experience of what it means to be a baptised and confirmed Christian. In the breaking of the word and the breaking of bread Christians remember God's pledge in Christ of everlasting love. In this remembering, the good news becomes a present reality.

And in participating in the communal celebration of the Eucharist, Christians recommit themselves in an ongoing way to their baptismal vocation and to the mission of their confirmation. They commit themselves to loving as they have been loved, to being the bread of life for others.

This suggests that Eucharist is something that all those present 'do'. In a former mindset it was something that the priest 'said' or performed, with all those present looking on as would spectators. But in the context of what has just been said about baptism and confirmation, all are celebrating the Eucharist together. Notwithstanding the distinctive role of the presiding priest, all are rejoicing in their baptism; all are committing themselves anew to their confirmed status in the Christian community.

THE VOCATION OF ALL

It is not just the word 'laity' that hides this universal responsibility. The words 'vocation' and 'mission', and even the word 'priesthood', also have this effect. Each of these three words has been narrowed down in its reference and the result again is to give the impression that all are not co-responsible.

The Word and the Experience

First the word 'vocation'. It is not that long since people such as nurses and teachers would have accepted the description of their work as a 'vocation'. It is not so long since we spoke of 'vocational schools', preparing young people for various trades. But such usages are disappearing. People do not want the word 'vocation'. It is too 'holy'. So we tend to use it only for priests and religious. We think of celibacy; we think of being set apart.

This feeds into the two-tier spirituality I spoke of above. A vocation appears as a further level of perfection within the Christian life. The renunciation involved takes the person out of the ordinary world of 'mere laity'. To the ordinary person, vocation is about somebody else.

The tragedy of this is that, while people do not use the word vocation of themselves, they continue to *experience* what the word refers to. The result is that they have no language for describing their experience. Their ordinary lives may be filled with self-giving and graced with all kinds of human qualities. But it has nothing to do with vocation. They are two different worlds.

Called by Name

Today, however, the fuller meaning of vocation is re-emerging. It is being seen that vocation is not a special call for some but the continuing experience of all. Listen again to the words of John Paul II. Each Christian is 'unique and irrepeatable.' God calls 'each one personally by name.' Each baptised person is 'entrusted with a unique task which cannot be done by another and which is to be fulfilled for the good of all.' 'Every disciple is personally called by name' (CFL, paragraphs 28, 33).

If people find the idea of vocation strange to them, at least let them accept that God calls each of us by name and that God has for each of us a unique place and purpose among his people. This 'call' is the fundamental meaning of vocation.

We could say simply that being a Christian *is* the vocation. Or more simply still, we could say that being a human being, becoming more of a human being, is what we are all called to. To be a Christian means that a person finds in Jesus the 'way' into his or her full humanity.

This means that there is nobody who is not called. It also means that being a Christian is never meant to be nominal but always meant to be lived. It is meant to carry a sense of 'something to live for, great enough to die for'. It is meant to feel like what the person in Jesus' parable felt on discovering a pearl of great price.

Some will still have in their minds the picture of vocation as a 'call' that a few receive at a certain moment in their lives. But this is confusing vocation with the particular *form* of vocation which some experience. Rather, all are called, but the call takes shape differently according to different lifestyles.

For most, their Christian calling takes shape in their married life. For some it takes shape in the single state. For a few it takes shape in priesthood or religious life. In particular, *Christifideles Laici* emphasises the 'secular character' of the vocation of the vast majority of Christians. Their vocation, in other words, is primarily about building the kingdom of God in the ordinary circumstances of their everyday lives (paragraphs 23, 34-38).

Called to Listen

Perhaps it would be more helpful to think of 'the call' in another way. It is not so much that God calls certain individuals, as that all people are called to listen to the voice of God in their experience.

> … from eternity God has thought of us and has loved us as unique individuals. Every one of us he called by name… However, only in the unfolding of the history of our lives and its events is the eternal plan of God revealed to each of us… a gradual process… that happens day by day… the fundamental and continuous attitude of the disciple should be one of vigilance and a conscious attentiveness to the voice of God. (CFL, paragraph 58)

Vocation is the call to listen. The voice of our experience *is* the voice of God. So we listen to our experience of life to hear therein the voice of God. Being called does not take us away from our ordinary daily lives into some 'religious' realm. It takes us *into* our ordinary daily lives, for that is where God is. It is a call to live our ordinary daily life more fully, more deeply, from the centre.

THE MISSION OF ALL

Like vocation, 'mission' has been narrowed down to refer only to a few. When we think of mission most of us think of the foreign missions and most of us probably know somebody who is or has been on these missions. It is they we suppose to be missionaries, not us. They are a bit like the soldiers off at war, we like those back home, keeping the home fires burning.

But if what I said about confirmation means anything, it means that mission applies to every one of us. All are 'called' (vocation) and all are 'sent' (mission). There is no need to labour this point as much of what is involved has been discussed in the first part of this volume.

There I spoke of God sending the Son and of the Son sending us. I quoted Paul, that faith comes through what is heard, through human communication. This communication depends on us - 'Christ has no body now but yours', as the prayer of Teresa of Avila puts it.

To be a Christian is to be on mission. It is to go beyond a narrow, privatised faith to accept responsibility for all. As John Paul II puts it, the Christian

> ... can never remain in isolation from the community, but must live in a continual interaction with others, with a lively sense of fellowship, rejoicing in an equal dignity and common commitment to bring to fruition the immense treasure that each has inherited. (CFL, paragraph 20)

According to the thought of this passage, mission is about community. It is the call to enter into community, with a sense of responsibility for building up the Body of Christ. It does not necessarily imply preaching or other activities that we associate with 'mission' and assume to be the job of others. It is more to do with the witness of a Christian life and a commitment to the quality of our life together.

THE PRIESTHOOD OF ALL

Even the word 'priest' belongs to all of us and not just to the ordained. This is stated clearly in the same second chapter of Vatican II's *Lumen Gentium,* and is taken up again in *Christifideles Laici* (paragraph 14). Prior to the ordained priesthood there is the universal priesthood of all God's people. This priesthood is theirs by virtue of their baptism.

The basis for saying this is in the New Testament where St Peter tells Christians that they are 'a holy priesthood, to offer spiritual sacrifices... a chosen race, a royal priesthood, a holy nation, God's own people, in order that you may proclaim the mighty acts of him...' (1 Peter 2: 5, 9).

It is not just the priest but all who are called to holiness. It is not just the priest who offers sacrifice; all, in the words of Paul, are to make of their lives a spiritual sacrifice (Romans 12: 1). It is not just the priest who proclaims the Word of God; all are called to witness to God in their lives. It is not just the priest but all who are called to build the kingdom of God on earth. In more technical language, all the baptised share in the ministry of Christ as priest, prophet and pastor.

Of course there is also differentiation between the universal and the ordained priesthood. But we are already well aware of that. What we have been less aware of is the way in which priesthood is common to all. This is a further indication of how impoverished our understanding of the 'laity' has become.

Conclusion

It was St Francis de Sales, I think, who once said that there is no more difference between the written gospels and the lives of saints than there is between written music and music sung. Somebody else spoke of the life of each Christian as being a 'fifth gospel'. Such images capture the depth and dignity of the vocation of being a Christian.

The basis for sharing responsibility for the life of the parish is a deepening of this sense of what it is to be a Christian. What lies at the heart of the parish is not some building. Nor is it the work that the ordained do. The heart of the parish is the lives of those baptised people who know they are loved by God, who listen for God in the voice of their experience, who feel themselves called to build up the Body of Christ. This is where the gospel is proclaimed.

It is only when we have transformed our understanding of 'laity' in this way that we can go on to clarify what concretely is involved in sharing responsibility for the life of the parish.

Resources

Themes of this Chapter	**Resource Material in Vol II**
The vocation of all.	*Called by Name*, session three.
The mission of all.	*Called by Name*, session five.
Being a parishioner.	*The Core Group and Parish Renewal*, session three, on the meaning of 'lay involvement' or 'lay participation'.

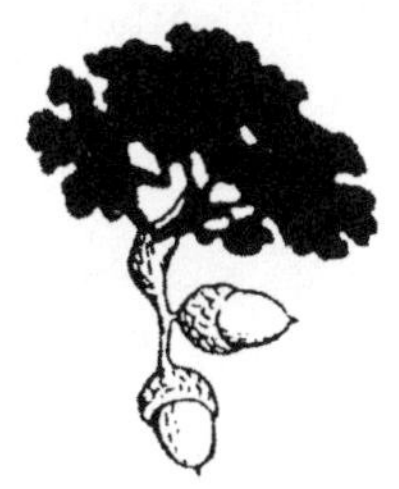

CHAPTER 9

The parishioner sharing responsibility

The main theme in reflecting on vocation, mission and priesthood was to bring out the responsibility of all God's people for their life together in the world. Now we need to break down this responsibility into different levels or expressions. For, not all are going to be members of parish committees; not all are going to be catechists or liturgists or choir-leaders; not all are going to help in the Vincent de Paul or the bereavement group. Yet all are responsible for the Church's task in the parish.

We can distinguish three expressions of this responsibility. The first, which I will call 'discipleship', is common to all in the parish. The second I will call 'ministry' and only some will become involved in this (though I realise that the term is sometimes used to refer to all the baptised). Fewer still will become involved in the third form, which I will call 'collaboration'.

As a context for this consideration I would recall what John Paul II said about the contemporary phenomenon of 'participation'. Speaking of our time as a time of 'humanism' he continued:

> The sign and fruit of this trend towards humanism is the growing need for participation, which is undoubtedly one of the distinctive features of present-day humanity, a true 'sign of the times' that is developing in various fields and in various ways... (CFL, paragraph 5)

Later he goes on to apply this to the participation of parishioners in parish life, stressing the indispensability of their activity in the Christian community (paragraph 27). His point is perhaps best illustrated by his use of the parable of the labourers in the vineyard (Matthew 20) in the introduction to the document.

The theme there is that *everyone* is called to work in the Lord's vineyard, that 'there is no place for idleness', that 'It is not permissible for anyone to remain idle'. The parish of the future, therefore, will be a parish of 'lay involvement' or 'lay participation'.

DISCIPLESHIP

Discipleship is what 'lay involvement' is most basically about. The terms 'lay involvement' and 'lay participation' often conjure up a picture of people doing things – being a reader at Mass or a member of the parish newsletter group or whatever. But being involved need not mean 'doing something' in this sense. For most people, in fact, it will not.

For instance, the most 'involved' person at Mass is not necessarily the person with an official function, such as the priest or the minister of the Eucharist or the choir-leader. The most involved person may well be the person who simply listens and prays and really feels part of something uplifting and important in his or her life.

Most people will never get involved in any of the specific kinds of activities mentioned in the last paragraph; indeed, many do not even want to. The involvement that is common to all, however, is the daily living out of the Christian life (or vocation) and the coming together to celebrate and nourish this at ritual.

To draw on some of the terms I used earlier, involvement is about being a 'practising Catholic'. It is about the meeting of spirituality and religion, the living out of a Christian spirituality in the ordinary circumstances of daily life, through quality of relationships and responsibility for others, through growth in understanding of faith, through personal prayer and community ritual.

Nominal or Real

Perhaps the most valuable aspect of using a word like discipleship is that it focuses on the differentiation between a Christianity that is nominal and a Christianity that is real. In doing so it tends in the direction of reserving the term 'lay involvement' for the latter.

For quite a number of people, Christianity would seem to be little more than nominal. Some such persons may be seen in church from time to time, but faith seems somewhat external or marginal to their lives. Others, while they would still refer to themselves as Catholics, never darken the door of the church apart perhaps from Christmas or the occasional marriage or funeral.

On the other hand, there are many others whose Christianity is quite real. It may be of a more traditional kind, expressed for instance in daily prayer and daily Mass-going. Or it may be more innovative, expressed for instance in participation in prayer or spirituality or theology groups. Or it may be a mixture.

But whatever the expression, there is a deliberate attention to being and becoming more of a Christian. Some learn more about this through adult religious education. Others have never studied formally in this way, but have learned what is involved 'on their knees' through prayer. Either way there is nothing nominal about it, it is a consciously committed faith.

Making these distinctions brings out the meaning of 'discipleship' and the usefulness of this term as compared to terms such as 'Catholic' or 'Christian' to denote members of the Christian community. For all the types I have alluded to, both those whose faith is nominal and those whose faith is real, can still be described as Catholics or as Christians, whereas only those whose assent is real could be unambiguously described as disciples.

This is because the words Catholic and Christian have become somewhat devalued in popular usage. 'Catholic' may be no more than a sociological description for many and the person referred to may have no more than a nominal faith. 'Christian' may sometimes mean nothing more than 'humanitarian'; for instance, people who have left the Church but who insist on the need for Christian principles and Christian values in society.

In contrast, the word 'discipleship' captures what may have been lost in these other two words. To call people disciples or followers of Christ suggests that they are taking Christianity seriously as their way of life. For such people faith cannot be a nominal matter on the margins of living. Rather, it becomes an aspect of all their living, permeating relationships, life at home, work. For somebody to be a disciple can only mean that Christ is at the centre of that person's life.

In this sense, John Paul II speaks of the need for integration in the Christian life between spiritual and secular aspects, between people's spiritual lives and their family, work and social relationships. There cannot, he says, be two parallel lives. Rather, 'a faith that does not affect a person's culture is a faith 'not fully embraced, not entirely thought out, not faithfully lived' (CFL, paragraph 59).

Giftedness

Discipleship takes people beyond or out of themselves. It takes them beyond a passive faith to a mature self-possessed faith. It takes them beyond an individualistic and privatised religion. It takes them out of themselves and into the Christian community. It expresses itself in a sense of responsibility for the life of the community, much as Paul spoke of individual giftedness existing for the sake of building up the community.

I use the word 'giftedness' deliberately, instead of 'gifts'. Speaking of the gifts people have often sounds like saying that so-and-so is good at, say, music or typing or administration or chairing meetings. In this sense there are lots of people who seem to be good at nothing in particular or who sense themselves to be so.

But giftedness refers to the human qualities a person has been blessed with. For instance, I might say to somebody; 'every time you walk into a room you bring joy'. Or I might say to another; 'you are such a positive force in a group'. Or to another; 'you have such a feeling for when somebody in the group is hurt or upset'. Or to another; 'how do you keep hoping when things are so hard?' And so on.

In this sense everybody is gifted, though differently as we saw Paul saying. Every human person lights up another aspect of the rich reality of what it is to be a human being. And in this sense discipleship is about people becoming more human, through the discovery and actualisation of their giftedness.

The most important challenge and task of mission in the parish is to acknowledge and to encourage this form of 'involvement', this basic expression of responsible Christian faith. It is this that all parish ministries and all collaborative leadership in the parish have as their end.

This can be forgotten amidst the practicalities or parish life such as building a community centre or doing something for the youth or caring for the needy. So it is very important to remember that the core issue for parish renewal is that 'religion' is sustaining and nourishing the 'spirituality' or discipleship of the people in the parish. The core issue is that the parish is moving towards a situation where *all are involved* in the sense intended here.

MINISTRY

As I use it here, ministry refers to a more specific, more public, more official involvement on the part of some parishioners. It is not for everybody and it is not lifelong in the way that discipleship is. A person may continue in ministry for a shorter or longer period of time.

The Variety of Ministry

In an active parish, ministry will involve lots of parishioners in all kinds of parish groups and initiatives, addressing themselves to all kinds of needs and possibilities in the parish. Recent decades have seen a flowering of such ministries, to the great enrichment of parish life.

Some of these ministries concern the Eucharist. We have ministers of the Eucharist, both at Mass and bringing communion to people at home. We have readers, exercising the ministry of proclaiming the Word of God. We have cantors and choirs helping all, in the words of Augustine, to pray twice as well. We have those who exercise the ministry of hospitality at the Sunday Eucharist. We have those who exercise the ministry of adorning and decorating the church and altar. We have the ministries of sacristan, altar servers, stewards and collectors.

A similar variety of ministry concerns the wider life of the parish. Some bring their catechetical skills to bear in providing for the further faith formation of adults. Some help develop a parish ministry to youth. Some exercise the ministry of caring, for the deprived or the lonely or the sick or the bereaved. Some assist in sacramental preparation programmes. Some build up the quality of communication in the parish. Some are engaged in the ministry of hospitality to newcomers in the parish.

These ministries will themselves change, as one initiative dries up and new responses emerge to meet new needs. Ministry, therefore, is creative rather than fixed and institutional. Its changing and emerging forms are the expression of a living parish.

Need for Clarification

Usage of the word ministry, however, requires clarification. Some people would apply the word to the priest and to the priest alone. They would hold that ministry pertains essentially to the ordained and that any other usage is invalid. Here we might refer to *Christifideles Laici.* While an indiscriminate use of the word could blur the distinction between the ordained and the universal priesthood, making for a 'clericalisation' of the laity, the document insists nevertheless on the diversity of ministry among God's people (paragraph 23).

Others would apply the word to *all* parishioners. Liturgists, for instance, would speak of the primary ministry at the Eucharist as the ministry of the assembly. Elsewhere we find reference to parishioners 'ministering' to each other in their ordinary daily lives.

Sometimes a particular book can confuse different meanings. It might begin by saying that ministry pertains to all God's people. Yet when it comes down to practical examples, the examples given concern public or official parish ministries – in which most people will never be involved.

Because of this variety of reference, I suggest using two words, discipleship and ministry. Two different words are needed because two different things are being referred to. On the one hand, there is the involvement that is common to all. On the other there is the more specific involvement of some.

Parish of Ministries – Ministering Parish

There is also a contrast drawn between a 'parish of ministries' and a 'ministering parish'. A parish of ministries means one where there are lots of groups and ministries in operation, all very efficient and organised. A ministering parish means one where each parishioner is aware of his or her vocation - what I have spoken of as living the life of discipleship.

It can happen that a parish is very good at the first of these and poor at the second. There may be a lot of well-run activity, but it may be quite church-centred and not touching a lot of people. Such activities can also be fragmented or compartmentalised, with little communication or coordination between them.

A parish of ministries can also be quite non-collaborative. It can

amount to little more than people 'helping out Father' in *his* ministry, no more than their being extensions of the priest and his ministry. In other words, a parish of ministries is compatible with a primarily hierarchical model of parish.

The conclusion I would draw from this is that the idea of a parish of ministries needs to be understood in the context of the more fundamental idea of a ministering parish. The ministering parish, the living discipleship of all, is the goal and the criterion of the parish ministries. Public or official ministries are at the service of the involvement of all God's people.

More than Delegation

This reveals a key aspect of ministry. All parishioners, and not just the priests, are responsible for the care of their Christian community. This is what discipleship means. Hence, ministry in the more specific sense is not 'helping out Father'. It is not delegated to people by the priest, but is something that people already possess by virtue of baptism and confirmation.

Delegation is what the term 'lay apostolate' may have meant, namely, assisting the priest in his ministry. If, for instance, the only reason for ministers of the Eucharist were a shortage of priests, then this would be an example of lay apostolate rather than ministry, suggesting that the only real ministry is that of the priest.

Ministry is something in its own right. It is a genuine exercise of adult Christianity, where parishioners take responsibility for their parish in specific, public, officially acknowledged ways. Therefore it is not to be treated in a patronising way.

Part of the reason for any difficulty found in mobilising parishioners for ministries may lie in this. People may resist involvement because they feel that this is the priest's work they are being sucked into. They may not have realised that being a Christian itself means being co-responsible for the life of the Christian community.

COLLABORATION

The terms collaboration, collaborative ministry, collaborative leadership, are usually reserved for a more specific form of ministry still. Here a small number of parishioners, together with the priests of the parish and with religious engaged in pastoral work in the parish, are involved in an extended parish team.

Perhaps 'collaborative leadership' is the best term to use, so as to differentiate it from 'ministry' in the sense proposed above. Also, I will use the term 'core group' to designate the group engaged in the exercise of collaborative leadership, though it may also go by such names as a parish team or parish pastoral council or parish forum or parish resource group or parish planning group.

The Overall Care

Whereas different ministries attend to specific activities or initiatives in the parish, the core group is concerned with the overall picture. It shares the responsibility for the overall care for the parish.

The Greek term *episkopos,* translated as 'bishop', is instructive here. The term means to regard or review or oversee, to pay attention to, to take care of. In collaborative leadership this task of overall care within the parish is shared. Or again, thinking of the term 'holy orders', the parishioners now become involved with the 'ordained' in the overall and future 'ordering' of the parish.

Even though very few will be involved in this collaborative leadership, it is intimately related to the responsibility of all. It is notable today that more and more parishioners desire to have a voice in their parish, to be listened to and to be consulted. A consultative spirit can be expressed in various ways – through use of the parish newsletter, or through a group preparing the Sunday homily with the priest, for instance.

But it is perhaps most strongly expressed through the existence of the kind of collaborative group I am describing here. The existence of such a group is a sign or symbol of the co-responsibility of all in the parish. In an ideal parish, perhaps all parishioners could meet together to reflect upon and plan their parish life. But numbers being what they are, the shared responsibility of all is channelled though the more specific shared responsibility of some.

Thinking Pastorally

There is a danger of thinking too canonically about such a group. Sometimes, when such a group is contemplated, priests fear losing power, through processes such as shared decision-making. But we need to think in pastoral rather than legal terms. We need to recall the story of Moses above, where the issue was not losing power but sharing the care.

Likewise today, as parishes enter the process of collaborative leadership and address the demands of mission in the parish, what is being shared primarily is the burden and responsibility. When we reflect upon it, such a sharing of the care makes for an increase in 'power', if power is understood more in terms of energy than in terms of having the last word.

As is the case with ministry, collaborative leadership is not a stop-gap measure to compensate for the reduced number of clergy. It is something that is right, because *the care of the parish is the responsibility of all the parishioners.* Perhaps the priest's own leadership role is best understood in this context. It is a leadership that encourages all to share the responsibility, a vital expression of which will be the sharing of responsibility in the core group.

But that sharing is not 'delegation', any more than ministry is lay apostolate. As one parish priest put it, how can you delegate to others what is already theirs? Collaborative leadership is right because the responsibility belongs to all.

Groups and Councils

At this stage some reference has to be made to the distinction I made in the first chapter between core groups, pastoral councils and parish councils. The essential distinction is between process and structure. What I am calling a core group focuses on process. The parish council, as that term has been used, is focused on structure. The pastoral council would seem to be somewhere in between (on pastoral councils, see William Dalton, *A Parish Pastoral Directory*, Dublin: Columba Press, pp 54-57, 260-261).

If the focus is on structure, members are usually representative of different areas or groups within the parish. There may be some form of constitution defining roles and procedures. But there may not necessarily be much already happening in the parish in the line of renewal. Structures are what people are thinking of.

If the focus is on process, structures come after. The concern is for the way in which the group relates. Process involves discerning who might be the right people for the group (i.e. not necessarily representative). It involves the group's learning to work together as a team, with a mutual appreciation of gifts and the articulation of a shared vision of parish.

It is a looser way of doing things, more reflective than administrative, with as much emphasis on *how* things are done as on *what* is to be done. For, the group is seeking not simply to execute tasks or functions, but to become itself something of what it envisions for the parish as a whole, namely, a living example of shared responsibility and collaboration.

OBSTACLES TO COLLABORATION

Such is the theory, but when it comes down to the practice there are many obstacles to the parishioners sharing responsibility. As the next chapter will be about priests, here I am interested in the obstacles within parishioners themselves. I will be concentrating on obstacles to collaborative leadership, though some of the obstacles to that will also be obstacles when it comes to ministry and even to discipleship.

'The Priest's Job'

First of all, there are obstacles concerned with how parishioners perceive the parish and the priest in the parish. In the traditional understanding of Church and parish, parishioners have a passive role. Because of this, when parishioners are invited to become involved in ministry or in collaborative leadership, they may react by saying 'that's the priest's job' .

This is to be expected since most parishioners are not used to being given responsibility, or to being acknowledged as responsible in the parish. They have not had the experience of any other kind of parish. Further, their experience of work in secular life can itself be quite hierarchical. So there is a general lack of familiarity with the kind of parish being envisioned today.

A Private Affair

Again, parishioners' spirituality may be of the privatised 'me and Jesus' kind, with little emphasis on the Church as communion. Or they may think of their religion as a personal affair, something not really to be talked about, something not demanding any public involvement beyond attending Mass

Because of this and other factors there may be a resistance to change. Nobody finds it easy to let go of what they are used to in favour of something they may not fully understand.

> Collaborative ministry asks those involved to be willing to change... This is difficult; people prefer the security of familiar ground... If collaborative ministry is to grow, the whole culture of pastoral life needs to become more positive about change and newness. (*The Sign We Give,* page 29)

Disillusioned

In other cases, parishioners have had previous experiences of attempts at collaboration and their experience has been disappointing. Perhaps the priest's own commitment was only nominal, so that the process never went very far. Perhaps things were going well until there was a change in parish personnel. In such ways people have been let down and have become disillusioned. They do not want to be let down again.

Even without there having been a previous disappointment, parishioners can suspect that the offer of collaboration is only a token. They may suspect that the priest has not really grasped the spirit of collaboration and that the process is not going to get very far.

Confidence and Competence

Some people feel a lack of confidence, which prevents them entering into collaborative parish work. They may feel that they have nothing to offer. They are not used to being active in a group and so may not think they would be able for it. There may also be a fear of responsibility.

Closely allied to this as an obstacle to collaboration is the extent to which people regard themselves as being not competent in this area. They feel the lack of theological formation. They may not have the familiarity with and training in the skills needed for collaborative group work. They may feel that they do not have the leadership qualities possessed by others.

These perceptions are often accurate. What is involved *is* something new. Confidence and competence in many cases have to be learned. What parishioners may not appreciate is that their basic giftedness as humans and their commitment as Christians is sufficient 'qualification'. These are what equip them to enter the *process of learning how* to share responsibility for the parish.

Time

Others are unwilling to become involved because they do not have the time. They have important commitments, at home or at work or elsewhere. They are already very busy people and they know that membership of a core group is a serious commitment.

In this regard, core groups can be unrealistic or unthinking in the time demands made on members. If this is the case, it can only increase the unwillingness of others to get involved. There is a need to be sensitive to people's prior time commitments and responsibilities and to draw on people insofar as this is realistic.

Peer Pressure

A final obstacle is peer pressure. Peer pressure, while often allowing for people's private practice of some form of spirituality, may be intolerant of any public identification with the Church. The experience of such peer pressure is not confined to young people.

What may we conclude from a consideration of these obstacles? Clearly there is need for encouragement, as well as for training and formation. But books and course do not change people in the way that experience does. What is needed most of all is that more parishioners would have the experience of themselves as co-responsible for their parish. In this there is also clear need for the invitation to collaboration to be genuine.

Resources

Themes of this Chapter	**Resource Material in Vol II**
Discipleship.	*Called by Name,* sessions three and five.
Meanings of lay involvement.	*The Core Group and Parish Renewal,* sessions three and four.
	The Priest and Parish Renewal, third meeting.
Core group and collaboration.	*Choosing a Model of Operating,* on choosing a way of operating reflective of the level of collaboration desired.
	Core Group Self-Evaluation.
	Working Well as a Group, on the skills required for working collaboratively

CHAPTER 10

The Priest sharing Responsibility

The contemporary theology of what it means to be a parishioner highlights the co-responsibility of all God's people for the care of the parish. Thus it points firmly in the direction of collaborative leadership between parishioners and priests. In this chapter we shall see how the contemporary theology of what it means to be a priest also points firmly towards collaborative leadership as the path forward for the parish.

To be a priest today is to be in partnership, both with parishioners, with parish sisters and with one's fellow priests. The days when the priest did everything himself and was completely in control are over. A new form of leadership is emerging. But the change is not easy and constitutes in fact one of the greatest difficulties facing parish renewal.

ADAPTABILITY

Any priest who has worked in a parish will know the experience of trying to be all things to all people. At one moment he is helping a couple select readings for their wedding, then he is shifting mood to preside at a funeral, then he is on his way home to prepare the Sunday homily.

The very variety of the demands made on the priest highlights a spirit of adaptability at the heart of his ministry. Adaptability is part of what it means to be a priest. It is a quality whereby he is responsive to the needs of particular times and places and persons.

It was St Paul who spoke of becoming 'all things to all people' (1 Corinthians 9: 22). As he describes it, he adapts himself to the different situations of different people in order that the gospel may be heard by them all. Such adaptability is far from being a mindless effort to be relevant. It is a complete subjection of self to whatever the preaching of God's kingdom demands in particular contexts.

It is the same spirit as Mary's 'Here I am, the servant of the Lord; let it be with me according to your word' (Luke 1: 38). Being a minister of the gospel means to count nothing as of value except what is demanded by God's purposes. It means letting go of what we may ourselves be attached to, if what we are attached to lies in the way of God's purposes being achieved.

Today, priestly ministry means letting go of certain ways of doing things. It means letting go of certain ways of seeing things. It means shifting from the attitude of 'this is the way we do things here' to the attitude of 'this is what needs to be done'. It means forgoing the building of our own kingdom and dedicating ourselves to the building of God's kingdom.

Reconsidering Priesthood

Part of the spirit of openness and adaptability is the willingness to reconsider priesthood itself in light of the times we are in. We need to reconsider priesthood in the context of the shift from maintenance to mission. We need to reconsider priesthood in the context of the turn towards collaboration. We need to ask; what are the implications of the turn to mission and collaboration for how we understand the priest?

Much time and many pages are currently spent debating the questions of celibacy and priesthood, of women and ministry, of the Eucharist in priestless communities. But there are also more fundamental questions. What does it mean to be a priest today? What is priesthood all about in today's context? What is the role of the priest in the new situation?

The urgency of these questions is reflected in the variety of expressions of priesthood today, but more importantly in the uncertainty that exists among priests as to what precisely they should be doing. In some priests the maintenance mindset persists, their identity and role revolving around administration. Others put the emphasis on evangelisation. Others again focus on activating the gifts that are there in the community. And others do not know what they should be doing.

HISTORICAL BACKGROUND

An historical perspective will help us to understand the significance of these different emphases and to articulate a viewpoint that can embrace them all. What I say here is quite brief and general, just picking out the main lines of development over the centuries.

Leadership

The first point of note is that the New Testament communities did not use the word 'priest' of any of their members. It is true that the letter to the Hebrews speaks of the priesthood of Christ; that Peter describes the community as a royal priesthood; and that priestly language is sometimes used in speaking of both leaders and members of the community. But no Christian is described as a priest. The two titles that are used are *episkopos* or 'overseer' (from which our word bishop) and *presbuteros* or 'elder' (from which our word priest).

While the word priest refers mainly to sanctuary, ritual and sacrifice, the words elder and overseer refer to leadership in the community. It would seem that, as far as the New Testament is concerned, it was the leader of the community who also presided at the Eucharist rather than vice versa (i.e. rather than presiding at the Eucharist being what made a person the leader of the community). We might also note again here the variety of ministries that existed in these communities.

Sacrifice

In subsequent centuries there occurred a shift from emphasising community leadership to emphasising cultic sacrifice. Partly this was due to the growing influence of the sacrificial language of the Old Testament. In the process the Eucharist came to be seen less as a meal and more as a cultic sacrifice. As it did, the one presiding at the Eucharist came to be called the priest.

With these developments a gap grew between clergy and laity. Just as in the Old Testament the priest was the man of the sanctuary, so too here the priest became understood as one who was set apart. His apartness was reflected in the way he dressed and in his celibacy. This fed into the emergence of the two-tier spirituality I spoke of earlier. It also fed into the identification of 'Church' with clergy and hierarchy.

Community Reference

By medieval times the identification of priesthood with sacrifice had reached the point where there was no reference to the community at all. Ordination was defined in terms of bestowing the power to consecrate the Eucharist. Such a definition allowed for the 'free-lance' priest, possessing a power, but with no necessary connection to any Christian community.

A comparison may be of help here. On the one hand, think of medical doctors. As a result of their training, they can be said to possess certain 'powers', namely, the knowledge and skill that enable them to heal people. But doctors are not tied to any community; they can travel and take their powers elsewhere. They can retire and still be doctors.

On the other hand, think of the president of the country. The president cannot depart for another country and continue to be president for this new people. A person is only president in relation to the community that elected him or her. Presidency does not travel in the way the powers of a doctor do. It does not continue after retirement. Presidency is a *relationship*.

By medieval times the priest was more like the doctor than the president. He possessed certain powers, regardless of any community reference. Nevertheless, when the priest was attached to a community, it was the fact that he presided at the Eucharist that constituted him as leader of the community, whereas in the early Church it was the other way around.

All this intensified in subsequent centuries, in an increasing emphasis on the cultic nature of the priesthood and an ever sharper differentiation of clergy and laity. Thus, priests who underwent their seminary formation in the middle of the present century (and even later) will testify that, as far as their training was concerned, the essence of being a priest lay in saying Mass and administering the sacraments.

A BALANCED PERSPECTIVE

This background gives us a greater appreciation of what is going on today. On the one hand there are priests whose identity is strongly focused on their sacramental role and on their differentiation from the laity. On the other there are priests who see their identity very much in terms of community leadership and community animation.

The Vatican *Directory on the Ministry and Life of Priests* is aware of both. It speaks of two opposite temptations for the priest, that of 'exercising his ministry in an overbearing manner' and that of 'eliminating all the differences... between the common and ministerial priesthood' (paragraphs 16-17). Some priests are far too conscious of 'I am the priest'. Others go to the other extreme and collapse almost all distinction between ordained and non-ordained.

Three Dimensions

A balanced perspective is one that can embrace what is valid in each of these tendencies. Such a perspective is to be found in the theology of priesthood of Vatican II's document on the Church, *Lumen Gentium.* Priesthood, both that of the baptised and that of the ordained, is seen from a Christological viewpoint in terms of the threefold mission of Christ as priest, prophet and pastor (though 'king' is used there instead of 'pastor').

The *priestly* dimension of the ministry of the ordained is not just about ritual. It is also about priests presenting their lives as a living sacrifice (Romans 12: 1). All of a priest's life is to be an act of self-giving. Its purpose is to build up the priesthood of all the community. Thus Paul speaks of himself as 'a minister of Christ Jesus to the Gentiles in the priestly service of the gospel of God, so that the offering of the Gentiles may be acceptable' (Romans 15: 16).

The *prophetic* dimension of ordained ministry refers not so much to teaching authority as to the proclamation of the word. This, according to Vatican II, is the chief duty of a priest (*Presbyterorum Ordinis,* paragraph 4). To this we can add that the greatest proclamation of the word is the Eucharist, so that in the Eucharist the priestly and prophetic roles meet.

The *pastoral* dimension is not primarily about power and authority, nor is it primarily about caring for the individual who is in need. It is primarily about leading the people, as a shepherd guides the flock. It is here rather than in the context of ritual that the language of sacrifice most truly belongs – in the good shepherd who lays down his life for the sheep (John 10: 15). Thus the priestly and the pastoral roles meet.

It is clear from this that there are three key dimensions to the identity of the priest and that the three run into each other. One has to do with the sacramental. One has to with evangelisation. One has to do with community leadership. An individual priest may focus on one rather than the others, but he may not neglect any. To the extent that any of the three is not prominent in the self-understanding of a priest, to that extent he has failed to understand himself as a priest.

We can readily see the problem with the word 'priest'. The word is meant to refer to the whole of the ministry of the ordained, but in actual usage it refers to only one of the three dimensions. As with 'laity' it is almost as if we need another word, almost as if the word 'priest', because of its historical accretions, cannot bear the weight of meaning being attached to it today.

LEADERSHIP: A FOCUS FOR TODAY

I said that no priest can afford to neglect any of the three dimensions. But if any were to be neglected, it is least likely that it would be the sacramental. Partly this is because the sacramental role is what figures prominently in the maintenance parish. It is the identity priests are used to. Partly it is because sacramental leadership is what people associate most with a priest.

Therefore the challenge for priests today is to build up the other dimensions of their identity and ministry, those of evangelisation and community leadership. This is the adaptation that is invited by the needs of today. *It is no coincidence that these two are intimately related to the themes of mission and collaboration that are at the centre of this book.* We have already seen the links between evangelisation and mission. As we go along we shall see more of the link between community leadership and collaboration.

In focusing the three dimensions for today, I would still see the sacramental as basic. This is what people associate most with the priest. The priest is the person who presides at the Eucharist. In that role he is the focus of unity in the parish. He gathers the people and in his person he focuses them on Christ. As one priest put it, the priest's role is to be 'the point of coherence' in the Christian community.

The problem now is that there are less and less people to be presided over. The clear need today is to form once more a Eucharistic community. *Christifideles Laici* (paragraph 26) says that 'the parish is a community properly suited for celebrating the Eucharist', but today the parish has to *become* such a community again.

Therefore it is not enough for the priest to define his role in sacramental terms only. The times as well as the theology demand that he be both a community leader and an evangeliser also. Thus the times are a time of grace for priests, inviting them into a fuller and richer experience of priesthood.

Collaboration

But there is one significant gloss to be added. Within the sacramental role, it is the priest and the priest alone who may preside at the Eucharist. But when it comes to building a Eucharistic community, when it comes to community leadership and evangelisation, the priest is not on his own, nor need he be on his own, nor should he be on his own. The burden of animation and evangelisation is a burden for which all disciples are called to be responsible. It is one that can and should be shared by the people of the parish.

Another way of putting this would be in terms of the idea of 'holy orders'. Ordination places upon an individual a responsibility for order in the Christian community. Today, this responsibility for order is not fulfilled by the priest bearing the burden alone. It is fulfilled in and through recognising and affirming the giftedness of others so that this giftedness might be put at the service of the common good. The priest fulfils *his* responsibility by inviting God's people to fulfil *their* mission of sharing responsibility for the life and future of the community.

In this way the theology of priesthood and the theology of 'laity' meet. They meet in the theme of collaboration-in-mission that emerges out of both the theology of what it is to be a priest and the theology of what it is to be a parishioner.

In this way too, clarity is possible today. Priests ordained in the middle of the century and later could say, 'I knew then what I was meant to be doing'. *But it is also possible to know today.* Today the priest finds his identity by entering into a shared responsibility with parishioners for the mission of the parish.

The Priest as Leader

Still there may be a suspicion that collaboration leaves the priest without any specific identity. This is not so; if anything, the priest's role becomes more important than ever. His new role revolves around the theme of leadership.

It is important to be clear what leadership means here. I do not mean leadership in the sense of 'a leader always emerges' in a group. In this sense priests may be just a cross-section of the community. Like the rest of the population, only some of them are 'natural leaders'. It is quite likely that there will be others on the core group who are more suited to leadership in this sense.

Nor do I mean leadership simply in the functional sense of animating a group or drawing out people's giftedness. This may well be part of a priest's leadership, but if it is all it involves, his suspicion of being left with no specific identity is well-founded.

The leadership I mean is a theological concept. It is, firstly, the leadership whereby the priest presides at the Eucharist. In this sense, leadership is a focusing of the people on what makes them a people, namely, the presence of Christ. This leadership is part of the definition of priesthood rather than a quality a particular priest may happen to possess.

Secondly, the priest's leadership is about the extension of this into the wider life of the parish. Just as the one presiding brings 'order' to the Eucharistic celebration, so the one in 'holy orders' has the care that all is ordered well in the life of the Christian community. This care means focusing people again and again on the heart of what they are about.

It also means focusing the giftedness and the wisdom that are in God's people. One way of expressing this is to say that the priest as leader is 'the moderator of the aspirations and plans and priorities of the community' (*The Sign We Give*, page 23).

Leadership Qualities

The first quality required for such leadership on the part of the priest is that he 'carry the vision'. The Christian vision must be alive in him; there must be a fire within. If this is not so, then he can hardly expect to keep the vision alive for anybody else

Secondly, the priest's leadership is about listening and empowering. In the past leadership may have been about a power residing in the priest. Today it is about the priest recognising and acknowledging the power that is among God's people, the Spirit in their midst. So he listens to detect and invite forth the power of people's giftedness.

This empowering also includes recognising and encouraging leadership qualities in others. There are probably others in the group who can, for instance, articulate the motivating vision, or who can keep the overall picture before the group. The leadership of the priest does not mean that these must always be his doing. His leadership, rather, is a concern that these functions get fulfilled.

Finally, the leadership of the priest is about being a constant source of encouragement. Collaboration between priests and parishioners is learned slowly. It suffers setbacks as well as enjoying successes. It demands patience and persistence. All of this in turn demands encouragement, the encouragement that keeps bringing the vision back to mind, so as to generate reassurance and new motivation.

It should be clear that, in this view of leadership, *relationships* rather than tasks are central. The leadership of the priest is at the service of collaboration and participation. It is not primarily about getting things done and getting people to do them. It is about a way of relating to other people and about facilitating a particular way of relating among people.

> If [the priest's] primary task is to enable communion to grow, rather than to 'run the parish', the relationships he develops will be central to his ministry. It is through the quality of relationships that he will most effectively invite people to make full use of their gifts and energy… He must be also able to let go of responsibilities and trust others with charge of various aspects of parish life and mission. In himself, he needs to be confident about a different kind of priestly identity… (*The Sign We Give,* page 23).

DIFFICULTIES WITH COLLABORATION

Priests Collaborating with Priests

It may sound strange, but the main obstacle in priests to the spirit of collaboration may have nothing at all to do with parishioners. The basic problem may well be about priests not collaborating with one another, either not being willing or not being able.

Sometimes an attempt is made to give theological arguments against sharing responsibility with parishioners. But it is far more likely that it is not a theological issue at all, but a personal and interpersonal one. If priests were able to work with each other they would be able to work with anybody. The problem is not about involving parishioners in collaboration, it is about involving anybody. It is arguably a matter of temperament and personality rather than one of theology.

The *Directory on the Ministry and Life of Priests* speaks strongly about collaboration among the priests themselves. Ordination, it says, means entry into the presbyterate, the community of priests in the diocese. It means that 'the priest cannot act by himself; he acts within the presbyterate becoming a brother of all those who constitute it'. Therefore he will 'make every effort to avoid living his own priesthood in an isolated and subjectivistic way' (paragraphs 25, 27).

It would seem that what is proposed here is far from the reality in most parishes. Many priests are 'lone-rangers', staking out their own territory with minimal accountability to anybody else. The reasons for this go back to the seminary, where many candidates for ordination somehow pick up a spirit of self-sufficiency and individualism which leaves them ill-disposed for collaborative ministry of any kind.

The Directory goes on to encourage some form of common life among the priests of the parish. In particular it speaks of priests praying together. Meanwhile, part of the parish priest's role is to promote common life and to consider curates as 'cooperators and sharers in the pastoral care' (paragraph 29).

Sometimes this is far from the reality. But if many parishioners feel that they are denied expression of their co-responsibility for the life of the parish, it may be some small comfort to them to know that quite a few curates are in exactly the same predicament.

Priests Collaborating with Sisters

Besides the difficulty priests have working with each other, there are the difficulties they have working with full-time sisters in the parish. Of course there are difficulties on both sides here. Sometimes a parish may be burdened with a sister who is not able for the job. But the more significant difficulty is that which sisters have with priests who do not seem to be able to work together with others.

Parish sisters comment that priests often have very little sense of partnership. This makes for a clash of mentalities between the sisters' own orientation to teamwork and the individualism of the priests. The result may well be that the full-time person who is doing the most creative work in the parish is the one kept outside the circle of those 'at the centre'.

To be fair, sisters may be at an advantage here. They have long since been forced to confront issues of mission and collaboration. So, when a sister begins work as a parish sister, she is already possessed of much of the mindset that priests are still struggling towards. However, it is a pity if priests see this as a threat to their position. It is, on the contrary, a gift inviting them into a new experience of ministry.

Priests Collaborating with Parishioners

When asked what are the obstacles in themselves to working with parishioners, priests list a number of factors. Some of these also apply to their inability or unwillingness to work with one another or with full-time sisters in the parish.

(1) First of all, they acknowledge that they were not trained for collaboration. It was a different theology of Church, of priesthood, of laity, into which they were educated, one in which collaboration did not figure. This is accentuated by what I spoke of above, the individualism which future priests begin to imbibe on their initiation into diocesan life.

The answer to this is twofold. Obviously some serious ongoing formation (or re-formation) in theology is greatly needed. But that alone will not suffice. I am reminded of what Cardinal Newman said, that as soon as we learn to shoot around corners, then we can hope to persuade people by logic.

In other words, it is not just an intellectual issue. People, perhaps adults particularly, change as a result of experience. The most important thing is exposure to the new mindset, to the experience of collaboration. New theological formation will be most effective in that context.

(2) Secondly, priests acknowledge that they are insecure with the prospect of collaboration. Hitherto there has been little accountability, little answerability – with the result that each priest can appear to be a law unto himself. If the priest enters into collaboration, he fears becoming vulnerable and being exposed in his inadequacies.

As those who have entered into collaborative ministry will testify, the fear is unreal, if understandable. Collaboration does mean vulnerability but it also means affirmation of a kind perhaps not previously experienced. However, it is hard to appreciate that from the outside. From the outside the priest is aware of his own underlying lack of confidence and wants to keep this hidden.

(3) Thirdly, priests are too used to being in charge. Many think, 'it's easier and quicker if I decide and do things myself' – which, of course, it usually is. Collaboration is slower and messier and many lack the patience for it. Or else they lack the trust for it. Collaboration demands trusting in others and encouraging the giftedness of others.

Not just that, but priests often cannot let go of having the final say themselves. Perhaps they fear the loss of authority. Perhaps their identity is too caught up with being in charge. Because of this they may stop short at 'delegating' tasks and 'consulting' others. But this is not enough. One parish priest recounts how he had to think again when he was told, 'you're great at delegation; what about co-responsibility?'

Again, many priests cannot listen to others in a way that takes on board what others are saying. They may think they themselves are the experts and that therefore they do not need to listen. Or else they may feel threatened by the diversity of new perspectives which listening would introduce. Or else they may think they listen when in fact they have already decided what to do anyway.

We have to be careful here to recall what was said above about leadership. To enter into collaboration is not to abandon leadership. If anything, leadership becomes more important than ever. Rather, to enter into collaboration is to let go of one kind of leadership for the sake of a better kind.

(4) Other obstacles have to do with time and energy. Many priests put a great deal of energy into parish administration and meetings. They shy away from the further meetings that the process of collaboration is going to entail. They resist the issue of redirecting time and energy that the mindset of mission raises.

At the same time, there are other priests for whom the problem is their lack of energy, even apathy. They seem to have lost their original motivation and vision. They show little or no interest in renewal of any kind. The presence of such priests emphasises the urgent need for ongoing personal and spiritual renewal.

Conclusion

In the end, it looks as if priests are in a similar situation to parishioners. Both have been familiar with a different way of seeing and doing things. Both find the way of collaboration unfamiliar and disturbing. Both feel inadequate, personally and professionally. Both have problems with time.

If this tells us anything, it is that parish renewal is about people rather than tasks. It is about people entering into a process of collaboration where they will experience change in themselves before they see much change in the parish. As far as I know, though, *nobody has articulated any alternative way forward.*

Resources

Themes of this Chapter	**Resource Material in Vol II**
Today's theology of priesthood.	*The Core Group and Parish Renewal,* session four.
Collaboration between the priests.	*The Priest and Parish Renewal,* second meeting.
Collaboration within the parish team.	*Parish Team Self-Evaluation.*
Collaboration with parishioners.	*The Core Group and Parish Renewal,* session four. *Core Group Self-Evaluation.* *The Priest and Parish Renewal,* third meeting.

CHAPTER 11

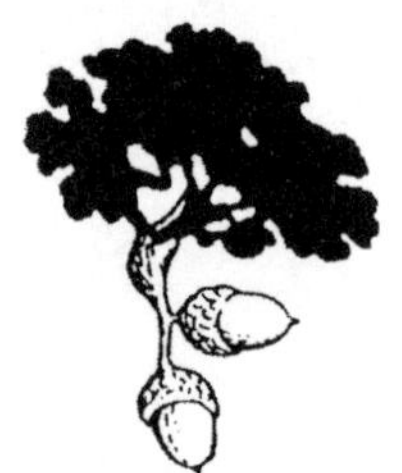

Process and the Core Group

When describing the experience of parish renewal in the Dublin diocese in chapter one, I said that the experience generally includes the formation at some stage of a group, comprising the parish team and a number of parishioners, that takes overall responsibility for the process of renewal. While this group can go by various names, such as the parish planning group or the parish resource group, usually it has been called the core group.

Because of the centrality of this group, it is in its functioning that the theology I have been outlining is most evidently reflected. It is here that the spirit and spirituality of collaboration is put to the test. It is here that the parish contends with the 'process' nature of renewal. Putting it another way, it is in the experience of the core group that the process of collaboration is *learned*.

This chapter gathers what has been learned from the experience in the Dublin diocese about the process of collaboration. What follows amounts to a kind of check-list which the parish core group can refer to when reflecting on the quality of its own operation. As will be clear, these factors focus on *how* the group functions as a group rather than on *what* activities or projects it takes on.

PROCESS AND PROGRAMMES

Parish renewal is about both 'process' and 'programmes'. More precisely, it is primarily about process, a process that will be assisted by programmes developed along the way in response to the emerging needs of the process itself. However, these two terms need to be explained.

Volume two of this book contains examples of 'programmes', for instance the *Called by Name* course or the *Spirituality for Today* course. Such programmes have a clear beginning and end. Participants know that the programme starts on a certain date and ends by a certain date, however short or long the period.

More significantly, such programmes are 'pre-packaged', composed in response to needs *elsewhere*. Of course the programmes are not 'set in stone'. Participating is itself a process that will take its own unique path, where the package will be adapted to local circumstances. Still, the broad lines have been laid down beforehand.

If parish renewal were itself a 'programme', then it would be a case of some kind of package being presented to the parish with the message, 'this is what you are to do'. There would be a beginning and an end, procedures and stages. But parish renewal is not a programme. It does contain programmes within it, such as those mentioned, but it itself is not a programme. It is a process.

A friend returned from missionary work in Africa gave a striking illustration. In the country where she worked, all the churches that had been built by the missionaries were scaled-down replicas of churches back home. But in one area the missionaries gave no model. Instead they worked on evangelising the people and building up the sense of Christian community. Then they encouraged the people to build *their own* church, with no plan other than what they themselves would devise as an expression of their faith.

The result, as can be imagined, was wonderful. But the contrast captures perfectly the contrast between working from a pre-set programme and working through an open-ended process. Either way, a church gets built; either way a task gets done. But the differences are huge.

Learning from Experience

Parish renewal has its objectives, along the lines of what I presented in chapter four about what a parish could become. And it has its 'way', the way of collaboration or shared responsibility. But within that broad context renewal is indigenous. Each parish and each core group works out its own way forward.

Many core groups, when they enter into the process of renewal, soon begin wishing that it were a programme rather than a process! They would like to be told what to do and what steps to follow. This is understandable as it is simpler and easier for a group to follow instructions than to carve out its own path with only general guidelines to help.

Parish renewal as a process can be compared to the course of a river. A river begins as a mountain stream, knowing only that it is going downwards, negotiating its way around rocks, then spreading out into a lake, then cascading, then evening out and slowing down, now straight, now winding. There have been many other rivers but there is no set course. Patterns are similar but each one is unique. So with parish renewal. The focus is not on following a pre-set pattern, but on *people learning from and being formed by experience at each stage.*

Thus one basic learning is the learning about process itself. The tendency is to focus on the *what,* to identify something to do and to become immersed in the doing. The danger is that this will become the *sole* focus of concentration. The group needs to learn that the *how,* the way it goes about its business, is at the heart of *what* it does. It needs to learn that learning is what it is all about – learning how to collaborate, learning to think in terms of process.

TASKS AND RELATIONSHIPS

There is a story told of the jarvey in Killarney who used to take tourists the long way around on the trip to the Gap of Dunloe. When asked why, he said that it gave them time to get to know each other better! The moral is that we are often better off taking the longer, scenic route in reaching our goal rather than the short route that bypasses togetherness, involvement and experience. This gives us time and space to overcome fears and to appreciate the giftedness of one another.

One of the most persistent challenges in parish renewal is the challenge of dealing with our tendency to be task-oriented. While any member of a group can be task-oriented, it can be of particular significance in the priest. If he is working out of a 'maintenance' mindset and if he thinks in terms of 'running the parish', then the task-focus is going to be very dominant throughout parish life.

I recall being a member of a committee that worked together for a number of years. At the end of the term it was striking how little we had grown as a group. We had got a job done but we had missed something on the way. We had achieved the task but we had not 'achieved ourselves'.

When a group is very task-focused as this one was, all the attention goes on getting something done and very little on relatedness within the group itself. As a result anything that is achieved is 'out there'. There may be a sense of satisfaction with the job, but little satisfaction as regards personal growth or change. People can even be hurt without it being noticed at all.

This points to a further aspect of 'process'. Parish renewal as process means investing in how people are relating and not just in the task at hand. Renewal is not simply a means-end affair. If it were, it might prosper quite well without collaboration. We all know the experience of feeling that everything would be much quicker and much more efficient if we just went and did it ourselves.

But in parish renewal *the goal is contained in the means*. It is a process of learning to be together in a certain way, both in the core group itself and ultimately in the parish as a whole. Collaborating is not simply a means to an end. The learning of collaboration within the group is itself an end.

In fact, by the way it seeks to be together as a group, the core group models in itself what it hopes will happen in the parish community. The vision is one of a parish where each person belongs, where the giftedness of each is affirmed and invited forth, where each grows in a sense of responsibility for all. The way towards realising this vision is through a process where the vision is already becoming a reality in the way things are being done.

LISTENING

Commitment to the relatedness of the group is a commitment to listening. Here I recall another committee where at a certain stage I was appointed secretary. Up to that point I had been contributing to discussions like everybody else. Now I began to appreciate the extent to which I had not been listening.

As secretary I had to keep quiet if I was to record faithfully what everybody was saying. Previously I often wished that somebody else would stop talking so that I could get my point in! Now I realised that many others were the same. An interesting point would be made, only to be buried by another interesting point. A heap of interesting points was building up but none was building on the last, because there was very little listening.

Real listening is difficult. We switch off when certain people start talking. Or we hear something and it is like a red rag to a bull; we lose touch with the speaker. Or we hear somebody out but with a closed mind. Or we hear something, stop listening and start planning the counter-attack. It can be rarely enough that one contribution genuinely respects and builds on the previous one.

On the other hand, if real listening occurs the fruits are undeniable. People feel appreciated. There are few experiences as dignifying as the experience of being listened to. People grow in trust. There is less need to struggle against others or to fear the agenda of another. Listening enables good, productive conversation to take place. It enables people to experience what being a person among persons is meant to be like.

Most important of all, if there is real listening then there is a chance that God will be heard! As one colleague put it, if people do not listen to others in a group, then they may not be listening to the Spirit. The equal baptismal dignity of each one means that nobody has a monopoly on wisdom. Only by each single person being listened to can we have any assurance that we are hearing the Spirit speak.

APPRECIATING GIFTEDNESS

Commitment to the relatedness within the group also means learning to appreciate diversity. It means recognising and affirming the giftedness of each person in the group. It means acknowledging that the Spirit works differently in each person. When this is happening, the group is becoming more of what it hopes the parish community will itself become – each person in his or her giftedness contributing to the upbuilding of all and to the unity of all in glorious diversity.

Very few groups are uniform. In most groups there are people who have different views and who take different approaches. For example:

- There are quiet, reflective people who say practically nothing.
- There are strong, forceful types who tend to take over.
- There are people who are very action-oriented and just want to get things done.
- There are people who could play with ideas and share their vision all year long.

- There are people who work from their feelings and who are constantly aware of how others are feeling in the group.
- There are planning people who want to get down to setting goals and targets.
- There are people whose concern, whenever there is conflict, is to harmonise the group rather than simply get caught up in the heat of the debate.

A group can be working against itself and frustrating itself if it does not bring such differences and diversity to consciousness. But if it does bring them to consciousness then it is enormously enriched. Now people know where other people are coming from. They appreciate that not everybody sees things the same way or goes about things in the same manner. They become grateful for diversity and learn to turn it to the advantage of the group. They eliminate the tension that results from not realising.

PRAYING TOGETHER

If I were to identify one element in the work of a core group that is indispensable, then it would be prayer. Meetings are made up of many elements – the initial chat, looking at minutes, debating issues, making decisions, breaking into small groups, listening to input, planning the next step, having a cup of tea. Any of these might be missing and the loss could be made up. But if there is no prayer, then a core group has lost sight of what it is about.

The reason is not that prayer makes a group function better, though it does. The reason lies in the nature of parish renewal. The work of parish renewal is the Lord's work, or rather our collaboration with God's saving work amongst us. So if prayer is lost everything is lost. The work becomes simply *our* work. As the psalm puts it, if the Lord does not build the house, in vain do the builders labour.

Sometimes people think that the ten or fifteen minutes of a two-hour meeting given over to prayer is ten or fifteen minutes of meeting time lost. Nothing could be further from the truth. The time given to prayer together is what gives the group its identity. This is not something that can be achieved with a quick prayer at the start or the end of a meeting.

In parish renewal people do not come together just to meet or to work. They come together to open their being together to the work of God's Spirit. They appreciate that in their context *collaboration is not a technique but a spirituality.* It is a world that is entered into through the gateway of prayer.

The prayer of the core group bears fruit in a number of ways:
- It focuses the group on the reason for its existence, the vision and the purpose that put everything else in context.
- It bonds the group in a single spirit.
- It creates a setting in which hopes and fears about parish renewal may be shared.
- It brings comfort when the work is difficult or discouraging.
- It challenges people when they are becoming complacent.

Prayer also teaches its own perspective on success and failure. It teaches the group to judge what it does in the context of what God is doing. In that context there can be great success in learning from something that has failed. And there can be huge failure in impressive results, when these have lost sight of the motivating vision.

ACTION AND REFLECTION

While there are many different personalities to be found in core groups, two contrasting types which keep surfacing are the predominantly active and the predominantly reflective person. One person could discuss endlessly the meaning of collaboration and the theology of mission and the vision of parish. Meanwhile there are others tearing their hair out in frustration and wondering, 'when are we ever going to get down to doing something?'

People who are predominantly active want talk to be translated into concrete initiatives. They sense the urgency of action and the need for results. People who are predominantly reflective want initiatives to be informed by thought. They need to tease out *why* this or that is being undertaken. They want time to be devoted to the requisite formation or training.

Every core group needs both action and reflection. If either is lacking, or if either dominates too much, the quality of everything suffers. If all the time is spent sharing and discussing, nothing gets done. The group becomes a talking-shop and eventually talks itself out of existence.

On the other hand, if the group plunges into action and gives no time to reflection, its activity lacks depth. The group may find it-

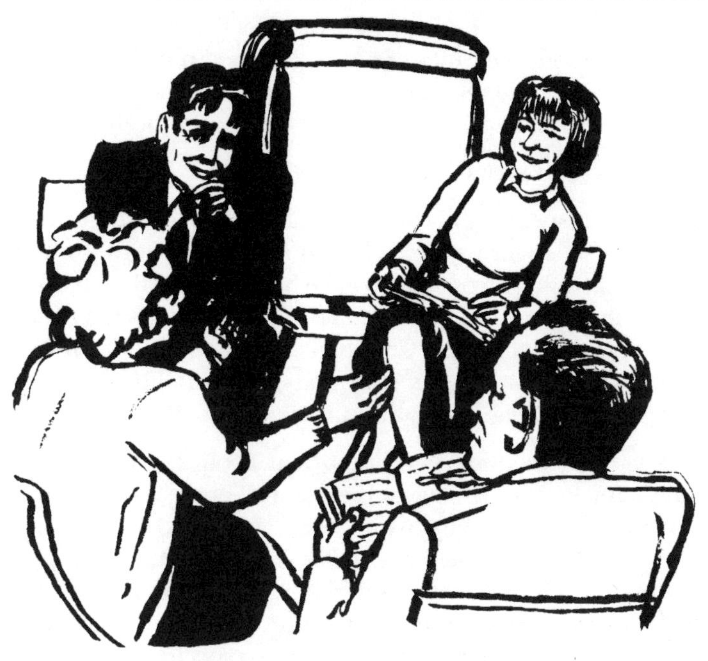

self regretting hasty decisions. It may dissipate itself in projects that lack any thought-out direction or ongoing review.

The word 'praxis' that is current in contemporary theology captures the synthesis that is desirable. Praxis refers to a lively interaction of reflection and action, of theory and practice. Action is informed by good reflection and it in turn raises new questions for reflection, in an ongoing cycle of action and reflection. Each group needs to learn and value the synthesis for itself.

Greater Depth

It is probably true to say that the greater danger in most core groups is that reflection will be neglected. Most people want to do something rather than sit around talking. In many groups there is a resistance to giving time to anything of a reflective nature, including further formation of the group itself, in theology or group skills or whatever else arises.

Nevertheless, experience has shown that core groups engaging in formation do fare better. They have more to give and their projects have added depth and direction. The group understands better what it is about. As well as that, reflection generates perspective, whereas the lack of reflection means that the group is 'scattered' in different directions and not 'collected' in what it is doing. And reflection affords the group the opportunity to grow in shared vision, thereby generating new motivation.

KEEPING AN OVERALL PERSPECTIVE

Earlier, when speaking of collaborative leadership in the parish, I referred to the word *episkopos,* from which our word 'bishop' comes, as meaning an overseer, one who pays attention to, has a care for the whole. I also spoke of 'holy orders' as a responsibility for the overall order in the Christian community. Collaborative leadership means that this care and responsibility is shared among God's people, just as the burden of Moses was shared.

This tells us something very important about the parish core group, namely, that its concern is the well-being and future of the parish *as a whole.* The boxing club is concerned with boxing; the Vincent de Paul conference is concerned with the needy; the liturgy group is concerned with the quality of liturgy; the newsletter group is concerned with improving communications. But the concern of the core group is not so specific. It is all-embracing.

But it is another thing to maintain this perspective. The danger is that, given the desire to get something done, the group will launch into some manageable project, only to find that it has become absorbed in the specifics and has lost sight of the overall picture. Instead of overseeing the renewal of the parish as a whole, the group is becoming simply another group ministering in the parish.

Looking Around

The core group can also end up in this position if it fails to attend to its relations with the various groups ministering in the parish. Others in the parish may simply regard the core group as just one more group among groups. Or they may feel threatened by it and regard it as an élitist group. Either way, the core group ends up being something other than what it was intended to be.

These things are less likely to happen if the core group is sensitive to other groups and supportive of their work. Ideally, other parish groups should feel affirmed in what they are doing, while appreciating the core group's role of reflecting on what else is needed to enhance the life of the parish. If this balance is struck, the core group will not be seen by others as arrogant, nor will it find itself having to apologise for its existence.

Looking Ahead

To maintain an overall perspective the core group needs, not only to look around at other groups in the parish, but also to look ahead. Becoming too absorbed in concrete projects also has this drawback, that it takes the group's attention away from the long-term and onto the immediate. This has to be resisted, as there is a constant temptation to think in terms of quick-fix solutions.

Parish renewal is about the long-term and the long haul. It is about planning ahead and establishing priorities. Other parish groups plan and prioritise for determinate areas of need. The core group concerns itself with the overall direction. It thinks in terms of the decades ahead and of *all* that is needed in providing for the future. A measure of its effectiveness is the extent to which it has entered into this mindset.

CLARIFYING ROLES

The core group will work harmoniously only if the respective roles of priests and parishioners are clarified. An illustration will bring home this point. One parish that took on the *Called by Name* programme (on the vocation and mission of all God's people) had come to the final session and the group was listing needs and priorities in the parish. They were in the middle of this when the parish priest got up and *told* the group what would be happening next.

Nor is that an isolated occurrence. It is a repeated cause of disillusionment when parishioners are led to think that genuine collaboration is taking place, only for it to emerge that the parish priest was not in fact committed to this at all. In the words of Cardinal Newman, his assent was notional but it was not real.

Therefore it is very important and only fair that people know where they stand and what they can expect. It may be that the priest is not ready for genuine collaboration and wants no more than a consultative group. It may be that he wants collaboration but within certain parameters. He may feel that, given his responsibility to the bishop, he must retain some control (not appreciating that core groups have always proved sensitive to the particular position of the priest).

At any rate, different arrangements are possible. What matters is that people are up-front from the start about the way things are really going to be. Too often roles are left vague. Forms of relatedness may be presumed. When it eventually transpires that there had been different presumptions as to roles and relatedness within the group, it can be very difficult to set things back on an even course.

It may well be that parishioners, when invited to participate, will make it clear that nothing less than genuine collaboration is acceptable to them, thus forcing clarity. It also has to be remembered that what changes people is not theories but experiences. It may well happen that a context of developing relationships of trust is what brings priests to a confidence about and a commitment to collaboration. If that is the way things are going, then something less than the ideal might be tolerable for a while.

> Collaborative ministry does not happen just because people work together or cooperate in some way. It is a gradual and mutual evolution of new patterns, new attitudes and new self-understanding, which will not happen by accident. It must be chosen and consciously pursued from conviction. (*The Sign We Give,* page 28)

SHARED DECISION-MAKING

An important aspect of the clarifying of roles is the question of how decisions are to be made in the core group. There is very little collaboration if the parish priest continues to have the final say in all matters. In contrast, there is a very high level of collaboration where important decisions are made by consensus.

Here both priests and parishioners have to look at themselves. Parishioners are so used to having the priest decide everything that many are quite content to go on like that. Others are so angry at years of never being consulted that they want a radical overhaul in the way things are decided.

On the other hand, some priests are incapable of making a decision and their indecisiveness blocks anything new happening in the parish. Other priests have to decide everything themselves. They are unable or unwilling to let go and to trust any matter of importance to others.

The ideal, which best reflects the spirit of collaboration, is what is called consensus decision-making.

> Many parishes and teams have developed a way of decision-making which is consultative in style. This form of decision-making brings wider resources to a decision than would be available to an individual alone. The more challenging option is aiming for consensus decision-making, in which the whole group or community works towards a consensus which becomes the decision. (*The Sign We Give,* page 31)

However, this form of decision making may not be necessary or appropriate for all decisions. It is certainly desirable for major decisions. But for less important matters a majority vote may be sufficient, or even the decision of a sub-group or of the leader of the core group.

The following are the elements involved in consensus decision making:
- The experience of each person is heard and taken seriously.
- Nobody claims or is granted a veto.
- The level of agreement or disagreement with a given proposal is named - the level for each individual and for the group as a whole.
- Consensus does not necessarily mean unanimity, but it does require that those who have reservations are willing to support the general consensus.
- If there is significant dissatisfaction in the group, or if one member has grave reservations, further research is indicated.

A group that makes major decisions in this way is clearly modelling the kind of participation and co-responsibility it seeks for the parish as a whole. But consensus decision-making does not come easily. It is most easily achieved in the context of a developing relationship of trust between priests and parishioners. Trust in each other and trust in the wisdom of the group assures all concerned that their views will always be listened to and taken seriously.

LEADERSHIP

The experience of parish renewal has shown that collaboration does not eliminate but if anything accentuates the need for good leadership. Collaboration is not simply everybody mucking in together. It includes the affirmation of gifts and one of the most vital gifts is that of leadership. The leader may often be the priest but not necessarily so. It may be part of the priest's role in the group to identify and affirm the gift of leadership in others.

Leadership in a renewal group is about somebody in particular who takes responsibility to keep the whole thing going. This includes what I spoke of above about keeping the overall perspective and the long-term in view. If nobody in the group is fulfilling this role the group will lose its bearings. If somebody is fulfilling it, the confidence and the sense of direction will be tangible. It may sound odd, but *a greater degree of collaboration and a greater degree of leadership go hand in hand.*

Keeping the Vision alive

Leadership, obviously, is far different from being in control or having the last word. The gift of leadership in the group is about:

- Keeping the vision alive and repeatedly bringing the group back to its motivating vision.
- Keeping the sights of the group from getting bogged down in the concrete and the immediate.
- Creating and sustaining an atmosphere of trust and mutual affirmation, where the Spirit can speak and be heard in and through each person.
- Ensuring that the focus on task is complemented by an attentiveness to how the group is relating.
- Making space for ongoing review and establishing criteria for evaluation and accountability.

CARING FOR THE CARERS

If a group becomes too pre-occupied with its own well-being it can end up doing little more than navel-gazing. But it is more likely that the opposite will happen, that in the compulsion to be doing something the group will omit to take the time to care for itself.

Time Commitment

There are two aspects to this care. The first has to do with time commitments. People involved in parish renewal know that, while the involvement may begin modestly enough, the demands start to build up. Some have the time and are glad to become more involved. But others have prior commitments that leave them with little time to give. In their case increasing demands can be unfair.

The well-being and harmony of the group demand that this issue be brought out into the open. Members should be free to state what time they can give and not feel guilty about not giving any more. The work should then be tailored to the time available, so that members do not feel over-stretched and pressurised.

This also applies to the length of time any individual stays on the group. This is something that should be negotiated. A staggered system of renewing membership, allowing for continuity, is the one favoured by most groups.

Ongoing Renewal

Secondly, caring for the group involves the group taking time for its own renewal. This is made problematic by the time constraints. In other words, because people have a limited amount of time to give, they are less inclined to give any of that time over to anything that is not 'at the coal face'. Some gentle persuasion, in the form of brief glimpses of what it might be like, is needed.

The ongoing renewal of the group includes further formation and training, such as theological reflection and development of skills. It includes time away together for prayer and reflection. It includes time for celebration. It includes time simply to get to know each other.

All of these tend to be neglected, even what seem like obvious matters such as getting to know people and having an occasional celebration. But to the extent to which they are neglected, the group is starving itself and impoverishing the quality of its contribution to the parish.

VOCATIONAL AND PROFESSIONAL

Taking all the headings of this chapter together, perhaps what it amounts to is a synthesis of the vocational and the professional. We tend to think of Church work as vocational and of the world of business as professional. We insist that Church work is the work of the Lord and we are suspicious of introducing too much of the business mentality. We would be slow, for instance, to speak of the Church as 'marketing a product'.

Yet both the vocational and the professional are needed in parish renewal. For too long we have hidden behind the vocational. The priest, for instance, can rely far too heavily on the fact that he *is* the priest and think that this somehow exempts him from putting the work in. For too long we have suffered from not having the criteria for evaluation and the procedures for accountability that are taken for granted in the secular world.

To synthesise the vocational and the professional is to say that, on the one hand, the work is the work of the Spirit and that we are privileged to be participating in something divine, the building of God's kingdom. And it is to say that, on the other hand, we are committed to quality in everything we do, that nothing less than our best is good enough.

Resources

Themes of this Chapter	**Resource Material in Vol II**
Check-list for the core group.	*Core Group Self-Evaluation.*
Process and programmes.	*The Core Group and Parish Renewal,* session five.
Tasks and relationships.	*Working Well as a Group,* session one.
Listening.	*Working Well as a Group,* session two.
Appreciating Giftedness.	*Working Well as a Group,* session three.
	Choosing a Model of Operating, session one.
Praying together.	*The Core Group and Parish Renewal,* session eight.
Action and reflection.	*The Core Group and Parish Renewal,* session seven.
Keeping an overall perspective.	*The Core Group and Parish Renewal,* session six.
Clarifying roles.	*Choosing a Model of Operating.*
Shared decision-making.	*Working Well as a Group,* session six.
Caring for the carers.	*The Core Group and Parish Renewal,* session nine.

Some practical indication as to how a group might pray together can be found at the end of the next chapter, as well as in *Hopeful Mysteries of the Rosary* in volume two. Also, much of the resource material in volume two suggests Scripture readings and/or a prayer service for the different sessions (see in particular *Working Well as a Group* and *Spirituality for Today*).

CHAPTER 12

Core Group meetings

Much of the work of parish renewal is done at meetings, most notably the meetings of the core group. It is here that the rubber meets the road; here theory and practice meet. These meetings will reflect the kind of collaboration that has been achieved in the parish. They will reflect the extent to which the ideal of the participation of all God's people in their parish is being kept in mind.

On this account, I propose to devote a chapter to discussing how the spirit of collaboration and participation may best be reflected in the way that meetings are run. There are three dimensions to this:

(1) Firstly, there is the dimension of running a meeting effectively. There are aspects of running a meeting effectively that are common to all groups which meet, from the Vincent de Paul conference to the company's board of directors. At this level the core group is simply getting its technique right.

(2) Secondly, beyond the level of technique, there are aspects of running a meeting which are characteristic of groups that are committed to the philosophy of collaboration. Only some groups are committed to this spirit and there are many effective meetings where this spirit does not come into play. At the same time, people in the world of business are realising that a spirit of collaboration and partnership makes for better quality performance.

(3) Thirdly, there are aspects of running a meeting that are specific to groups which are Christian. Thus, for the core group, there is more to a successful meeting than simply getting things done. Because the group is Christian, there is even more involved than getting things done in a spirit of collaboration. Things must also be done in a way that is specifically referred to

Christ. At this level the core group is seeking to be faithful to its Christian calling.

This chapter will discuss all three dimensions. I might also mention that the discussion will involve some repetition of points covered in the previous chapter.

The What and the How

Before discussing the three dimensions, it will be helpful first to advert to some of the things that can irritate and exasperate people about meetings. For instance:
- Even though the meeting is supposed to be an exercise in collaboration, the person in the chair (usually the priest) makes all the decisions.
- People arrive expecting an open discussion, only to find that matters have been sewn up beforehand.
- The meeting is being run by somebody who is unacceptable to the group.
- The meeting starts late; people are still drifting in some time into the meeting.
- The meeting seems to go on and on and lasts well past the agreed finishing time.
- There is either no prayer or else a hurried mumble at the start or the end; it is felt that anything more would encroach on the time for the meeting.
- The meeting has not been planned or prepared for properly.
-There is no shared understanding of what the purpose of the meeting is; people have different ideas as to what the meeting is all about.
- The meeting is dominated by one person or by a few people; they keep talking and intervening, with the result that others never contribute.
- There is hardly any real listening, one point gets piled up on top of the last, as people seem to be concerned only with what they themselves have to say.
- People feel they are not being listened to or not taken seriously.
- The agenda is too rushed and there is no time for reflection.
- The meeting is being undermined by personal agendas, interpersonal animosities, power struggles.
- Disagreements are not sorted out and are left festering.
- Some members of the group are proving very difficult.
- Decisions are never followed up.

- The meeting is just a talk-shop; no action is ever taken.
- The group is either too big or too small for the task in hand.
- The venue is uncomfortable.

Such issues as these highlight the difference between the *what* and the *how* of the meeting, the content and the process. In nearly all of the above, the problem is the *how*. The problem is not *what* is being discussed or *what* is decided, but *how* people go about discussing and deciding.

In the last chapter I emphasised how a strong task-orientation can make for a failure to invest in relatedness. The point here is in the same vein. A parish renewal meeting usually has a task (though some do not even have that much). The meeting might be quite efficient in going about the task. But a meeting could be run quite efficiently and yet betray the spirit of parish renewal. Priests, and sometimes parishioners too, can find this hard to grasp. A meeting can be run with total efficiency and yet be a total failure.

GETTING THE BASICS RIGHT

At the same time there are meetings which do not seem even to have efficiency as a criterion. As well, there are meetings which genuinely strive to practise collaboration, but which are frustrated because of failings at the level of efficiency. So, recalling the causes of exasperation listed above, it is worth identifying the elements that make for an efficiently-run meeting.

Since there are ten in what follows, let us call them the 'ten commandments' for a well-run meeting. If a core group commits itself to operating in a Christian way, in a collaborative way and in an efficient way, then these are the criteria for efficiency. I would recommend that the group should, very early on in its life, explicitly contract itself to observing these commandments, and that it should arrange for some way of periodically 'examining its conscience'.

1. *Meetings should start and end at the agreed times.* Normally, there is no reason why meetings should last longer than ninety minutes – and every reason why they should not last any longer. People lose concentration; they become tired and irritated; they make hasty and rash decisions; they are late for their next appointment. They also stop looking forward to meetings.

2. *The task of each meeting should be clearly understood by all present.* It has been said that 60% of meetings fail in this regard. The result is that people are working at cross-purposes; eventually nobody is sure what is going on. Not only should the overall purpose of the meeting be clear, but also the purpose of discussing each item on the agenda. Some items are for information, some for clarification, some for an initial brainstorming, some for an open-ended discussion, some for decision.

3. *The task should be worthwhile and should be felt to be worthwhile by those present.* Sometimes people can be at a meeting merely out of fidelity. They do not really see the point in, nor are they motivated by what is being discussed. If this is the case, discussions are clearly going to be lifeless and participation is going to be low.

4. *The agenda should be well-prepared.* If there are too many items, some will receive all the attention and others will be rushed through. If a packed agenda cannot be avoided, a definite amount of time should be assigned to each item and this should be rigidly adhered to. If the discussion goes off on a tangent, it should be brought back on course immediately.

Items on the agenda should be sequenced in the most appropriate way. There are arguments for dealing with the most important items *either* first *or* last *or* in the middle. There is something to be said for alternating between heavier and lighter items.

5. *The environment should be right.* Many meetings are ruined because the room is too hot or too cold, or because the seating is uncomfortable or badly arranged, or because the place is too dark, or because there are repeated interruptions. Sometimes it is not possible to do anything but most times it is. If the task is worthwhile, the group is entitled to work in conditions that reflect this.

6. *There should be clarity concerning roles.* It should be clear who is responsible for preparing the meeting, who notifies participants, who chairs the meeting, who records (and whether this person takes minutes or simply records decisions). It should be clear how decisions are made and what say each of those present possesses. People should know if they are there to be informed, or to be consulted, or to share in the decision-making.

7. *The frequency of meetings should be right.* There should be enough meetings in order to get the work done. At the same time, if the people involved are there in a voluntary capacity, the time commitment has to be reasonable and realistic in the light of other demands on their time. While it can be difficult to get the balance right, regular review will at least ensure that people's feelings are being consulted and considered.

8. *There should be a proper follow-up to meetings.* Frustration is the result when, after an item is discussed, the chairperson passes on to the next item without a clear conclusion having being reached. Likewise, frustration is inevitable when a meeting makes a number of decisions but does nothing to ensure that these decisions will be implemented.

Time should be set aside before the end of each meeting to clarify with regard to each decision: who is to do what, and when? It helps keep the pressure on if a record of this is circulated to each member soon after the meeting.

9. *There should be time to socialise.* If everybody just arrives in, sits down to work, concludes and goes home, the work may be done but the joy will go out of it. People need to get to know each other if they are to work well and happily as a group. The chat, the cup of tea, the occasional social event, are no mere appendages.

10. *There should be evaluation.* At agreed intervals, for instance once every year, the performance of the group should be evaluated. This might be done by the group itself or by somebody outside the group acting as facilitator. If it is done by the group itself, outsiders might be called upon to assist, for instance by providing instruments for evaluation. However, if there is no evaluation, the group cannot really answer the question, 'how well are we doing?'.

THE SPIRIT OF PARTNERSHIP

Such are the criteria for the group's working in an efficient way. The core group may well wish to modify or refine the criteria in the light of its own experience. But efficiency is not enough in a core group. Part of its very reason for existing is to operate in a collaborative way, thereby practising what it proclaims.

The aim is that the spirit of partnership and collaboration would dominate at all times and at all stages of the group's operating. This is not achieved overnight; it has to be learned. Therefore it is important that the group comes to appreciate that its role is not just one of performing tasks, but also one of *learning how* to be a group permeated by the spirit of collaboration.

It is desirable that this 'learning how' be accepted explicitly by the group as its own agenda from as early on as possible in its existence. This acceptance will be most concrete when the group accepts or contracts that its meetings will be pervaded by the spirit of collaboration.

This applies, first of all, to the preparation of the meeting and its agenda. Many meetings are prepared by only one person. As a result the direction of the meeting is owned by only that person. The rest may feel relatively passive. They may think that their role is to 'help Father' with his work.

Some will feel angry rather than passive, especially if they discover that everything has been sewn up before they start. But in general, there may be an unspoken disquiet if there has been no opportunity for a common agenda to be built up, whereby what is discussed at meetings reflects the concerns of each person in the group.

How to run Meetings

To make concrete the spirit of collaboration, the core group should decide together how meetings are actually going to be prepared and run. For example, the group might consider the following four possible options:

(1) The meetings are prepared and run by the chairperson, in conjunction with the secretary.

(2) The chair rotates, whether every meeting or annually or something in between, with the secretary constant so as to ensure continuity. Again, there might be a permanent organising secretary, with a different person taking minutes at each meeting.

(3) A planning group is established, say for a period of one year, with the responsibility for preparing and running the meeting during that time.

(4) The planning group system is adopted, but on a rotating basis, a new group taking over perhaps every few months, perhaps even for each meeting.

The choice should be made in a spirit of deliberation. In deciding which option is best for the group at this time, the group should be able to say how the option chosen is meant to forward the spirit of collaboration.

The Participation of All

The spirit of collaboration must also pervade all aspects of the experience of the meeting itself. More than anything else, this means ensuring the real participation of all at all levels, from discussing to deciding. The real participation of all is based on the acceptance that each member of the group has an equal part to play, and on an appreciation of the giftedness which each brings to the group.

In the last chapter I highlighted the importance of listening and of appreciating diversity. These are two important ways in which collaboration will be evident in the running of meetings. Listening means that all are involved, all are affirmed, all are given voice. It means that contributions build on each other, as opposed to being piled on top of each other. It means an end to domination by any person or group or interest or agenda.

Appreciating diversity gives the meeting an air of inclusiveness. Different personalities, perspectives, views, spiritualities are welcomed. Minorities are invited into speech and minority views are taken seriously. The quiet are heard no less than the talkative. This means an end to the intolerance of difference so destructive of collaboration.

In the last chapter I also highlighted the value of consensus decision-making in making collaboration real. Indeed, the way decisions are made is one of the best indicators of the quality of collaboration. Commitment to consensus means trusting in the collective wisdom of the group. It means that all contract into the process of reaching consensus.

There was one parish meeting where, on a particular issue, the group was split, 60%-40%. When the figures were announced, the majority proclaimed 'we won!' That is the opposite of the spirit of consensus. Consensus means that the majority do not take the minority view lightly. And it requires that the minority who disagree are willing to go along with the greater wisdom.

Conflict

Finally, the spirit of collaboration makes for a creative approach to conflict in the group. Essentially, this approach sees that conflict itself is not the problem. It understands that conflict is residual in human affairs, that differences of opinion or clashing viewpoints are natural. Conflict and clashes, therefore, will be part of the life of any group.

The problem is not the difference or the difficulty itself, but the way in which it is handled. The spirit of collaboration encourages the development of the personal skills necessary for handling conflict in a way that is creative and to the advantage of the group. Such skills include:

- Learning to understand the other, to stand in the other person's shoes and to see things from that perspective.
- Depersonalising sensitive issues, so that points can be debated without persons being attacked.
- Learning to be assertive without being aggressive.
- Working to establish a common commitment to resolve the difficulty.
- Looking for win-win rather than win-lose outcomes.
- Building common ground by establishing points of agreement.
- Being willing to make concessions in order to advance agreement.

In summary, the spirit of collaboration is promoted if
(a) The group explicitly sees the learning of collaboration itself as a foremost aspect of its task.
(b) The group chooses a mechanism for preparing and running

meetings that reflects the co-responsibility of the whole group. (c) The group commits itself, in the process of the meeting itself, to the values of listening, of appreciating difference, of deciding in a spirit of consensus, and of resolving conflict in a creative, group-building way.

CHRISTIANS IN GROUPS

Besides committing itself to operating in an efficient way and in a collaborative way, the core group commits itself to operating in a Christian way. For it is not just that collaboration is at the heart of the life of the group. It is that being *Christians* in collaboration is the heart of its life.

This is not meant to imply that Christians collaborate in a different way from others but, rather, that being Christians adds a distinctive motivation to the group's practice of collaboration. For Christianity is not indifferent to the spirit of collaboration. As we saw in chapter seven, collaboration is at the heart of Christianity itself. Therefore the fact that they are Christian should intensify people's commitment to collaboration. Let us apply this to the themes above.

Collaborative meetings are ones where there is participation by all and where listening means that all voices are heard. This brings to mind the God of Jesus Christ, the God who hears the cry of the poor just as he heard the cry of the people in Egypt, the God of the lost sheep and the lost coin and the lost son. Belief in such a God can only mean a passion for the inclusion of all.

Collaborative meetings are ones where decisions are made collectively, with a trust in the common wisdom of the group. This brings to mind the God who does not save us without our own participation, who does not decide our future for us, but invites us into a process where God and ourselves carve out our future together. God's 'letting go' in such an act of trust in humanity can only inspire Christians to a similar trust in the power of one another.

Collaborative meetings are ones where conflict is dealt with in a creative and upbuilding way. This brings to mind God's way with us in responding to the sin of the world. God's way was not that of punishment, nor that of exerting a greater force, nor that of vengeance. God's way was the way of the cross, the 'powerfulness of defencelessness', inviting us back into communion and into new life. Disciples of Christ bring the same spirit to bear whenever they experience conflict in their life together.

These are just indications of how the 'way' of collaboration and the 'way' that is Christianity resonate with one another. What they suggest is that Christians should fit easily into collaborative contexts because the dynamics of collaboration are already so much part of Christianity. Putting it more bluntly, if Christians resist or undermine the collaborative process, they are also resisting and undermining something of what they themselves are.

Prayer

This brings me back, finally, to the topic of prayer already discussed in the last chapter. Their prayer together is where Christians *do* collaborate in a way that is different from that of others. Others may collaborate but they do not pray. For Christians prayer is what brings into focus the centrality of their Christianity. Prayer is the centre of their meeting.

When they pray together, the members of a core group avow who they are. They avow the Christianity that is the core of their humanity. In praying they share both their uncertainties and their convictions, their questions and their struggles. In this way they bring their partnership to a new interpersonal depth.

When they pray together, the members of a core group open themselves to what is greater than themselves, so as to listen to its wisdom and logic. In this way they open their collaboration to the greatest depth of all. Their collaboration becomes a collaboration in the Lord and with the Lord. They themselves become part of the divine-human collaboration that is the story of salvation.

The only way in which to understand and appreciate this is to do it. It is the prayer itself, carried out with commitment and consistency that reveals its own significance and value. People come to see that their work, their collaboration, has entered into a new dimension that makes it quite different from any other exercise in collaboration.

It may help to conclude with some concrete illustration. I suggested above that an ordinary core group meeting might last for about ninety minutes. I would now suggest that prayer should take up the first ten or fifteen minutes of the meeting. Anything less is not taking prayer seriously enough; the divine dimension of collaboration will not shine through. Anything more is unnecessary. In addition, the group will do well to arrange days or afternoons of prayer and reflection once or twice a year.

One simple (and flexible) structure for the time of prayer would be the following. A different member (or a couple of members) of the group takes responsibility for the prayer at each meeting. It helps if the text of the prayer can be duplicated for everybody. Then:

(a) Prepare a 'sacred space' in the room; this can be something as simple as a lighted candle on the floor, or it can be more elaborate.

(b) Begin with a few moments silence in order to focus attention.

(c) The group might sing, or listen to music, or else recite together a prayer that introduces the overall theme of the reflection.

(d) There follows a reading/meditation, from the bible or elsewhere.

(e) A period of silent prayer.

(f) An opportunity, for anybody who wishes, to pray or reflect aloud.

(g) There might be a litany, or a series of prayers of the faithful, to be read one per person.

(h) Concluding prayer said together.

Resources

Themes of this Chapter	Resource Material in Vol II
Effective meetings.	*Working Well as a Group*, session seven.
Conflict at meetings.	*Working Well as a Group*, session four.
Prayer at meetings.	*The Core Group and Parish Renewal*, session eight.
Evaluating meetings.	*Core Group Self-Evaluation.*

Group Meetings that Work: A Practical Guide for Working with Different Kinds of Groups (Slough: St Pauls, 1994), by Catherine Widdicombe is a very practical book, full of the wisdom of experience. It will be particularly valuable for the leader of a core group.

CHAPTER 13

Looking ahead

The Distance Travelled

Again and again at parish renewal meetings, parishioners voice their concern regarding 'the youth' and 'the marginalised'. As they do, they show their awareness of the great challenge presented to the church today. More and more people ceasing to be involved, young people particularly, casts a shadow over the future.

Measured against this concern, parish renewal might seem to have achieved little so far. But I wonder if it is not an unfair way of measuring success. Looking back now over the ten years since the present process was initiated in the Dublin diocese, we can see that a great distance has in fact been travelled. Perhaps the best way to put it would be to say that the progress made has been modest but profound.

With hindsight it is obvious that the first concern of parish renewal would have to do with those *still* involved in the life of the parish, both parishioners and priests. As has come up repeatedly in the previous chapters, the change of mindset required on the part of those still involved is a huge challenge in itself. It takes a great deal of time, years even. After ten years it is still the main issue to be negotiated for many.

It is very clear now that parish renewal is a long, ongoing process. We have to learn to think in terms, not of months or years, but of decades. It is also quite clear that we are still at an early stage. Most of the energy up to now has gone into establishing the principle or spirit of collaboration.

It is only as that spirit is established that groups can begin to address the larger challenge of mission and evangelisation. Perhaps the most accurate assessment of the present situation in Dublin would be to say that the principle of collaboration is becoming more and more widely accepted; that it should not be too long before its acceptance is universal; and that, where it has been accepted, parishes are beginning to address the challenge of 'the new evangelisation'.

EMERGING TRENDS

From this perspective, what has been presented in the previous twelve chapters is simply a marker, indicating the journey travelled so far. In ten or twenty or thirty years time very different books will be written about the further developments that as yet can hardly be envisaged. At the same time there are some signs in evidence which hint at what the next stages in the process might be.

These signs have to do mainly with the undeniable fact that parish renewal along the lines presented in this book is being accepted as the way forward by more and more parishes. The implications of this are being felt in two areas in particular, that of diocesan policy and that of the provision and appointment of resource personnel.

The Diocese

As regards the diocese, it is clear that parish renewal is coming more and more to the centre of diocesan policy and planning. While it was initiated 'from above' in the mid-1980s, the movement has grown 'from below', from the parishes. As it has grown, it has been proven by its fruits. This in turn is the opportunity for a new initiative from above, from the diocese as a whole.

One illustration of this is in the area of diocesan appointments. There is a fear in parishes that the process of renewal could falter and even collapse with a change of parish personnel. This raises an issue for those responsible for appointments and there are signs that the issue is being addressed.

We are now at the point where the importance of the process of parish renewal is being felt in the appointment of priests. A criterion is emerging of appointing priests who can tune into and support the process of renewal. Not only that, but there is a growing expectation at diocesan level that priests *should* be supportive of parish renewal. There is a new sense of answerability or accountability emerging.

This is also reflected in a growing expectation on the part of the diocese that each parish should have in place some form of parish pastoral group whose purpose is to attend to the need for renewal. Parish renewal remains indigenous and dependent on local motivation. But increasingly, an indigenous process fired by local motivation is being seen as the *norm*.

Resource Personnel

The second trend has to do with resource personnel. At this point there is no question as to the proven value of the full-time coordinators working in the diocese, as well as of the resource persons who help in meeting the needs that emerge in the parishes.

The logic of this would seem to be 'more of the same'. The presence of the full-time coordinators and of the resource persons has made possible advances that could hardly be contemplated otherwise. More full-time and part-time personnel can only have the effect of making for further advances still.

Here I would recall again the large number of men and women who have, of their own volition, become qualified in various areas of theology and ministry, and who wish to apply their gifts to the needs of the Church. It would seem that we are approaching the time when there will be more and more full-time, non-ordained persons working in the area of parish renewal.

Perhaps this will emerge gradually. There may be part-time appointments before there are full-time. There may be personnel appointed to work with clusters of parishes before there are personnel appointed in individual parishes. But the direction seems clear.

A first step in this direction might well be the proper acknowledgment of the non-ordained who are *already* working in full-time parish ministry, namely, the parish sisters. Already they are engaged in addressing the needs of an evangelising parish, but frequently without due recognition. That they take their place within truly collaborative parish teams is clearly indicated.

A CONCLUDING ANALOGY

I would like to conclude this volume with one overall reflection on the significance of parish renewal for the life and future of the

Church. I will do this by drawing an analogy between the growth of modern science and the growth of parish renewal.

I recall once reading a book about the origins of modern science. The theme of the book was that what we know as modern science did not appear overnight, but only as the outcome of a development stretching over a period of some four hundred years, from around 1300 to towards the end of the seventeenth century.

Up to the middle ages the dominant science had been Aristotelian. But around 1300 there began a movement away from a metaphysical towards an empirical basis for science. Scientific method now pivoted upon empirical observation, hypothesis and verification.

As it did, new discoveries multiplied. But they could not be expressed adequately because there was no overarching system to incorporate them. This made for tension, as the new discoveries did not sit easily with the old system. The case of Galileo is illustrative of this. But eventually, towards the end of the 1600s, the new ideas had accumulated to such a degree as to bring forth a new system capable of supplanting the old – the system we know as modern science.

This suggests a way of bringing together what I have been saying about parish renewal over the last twelve chapters. Until a few decades ago, a system of ideas, a set of practices, a way of doing things, had been in place for quite a long time. Then new insights, practices, procedures began to emerge. Vatican II was a watershed in this regard.

But, as in the case of modern science, the new developments did not always sit easily with what had gone before. New initiatives were emerging, but within the context of an older structure. It is only when the new insights and initiatives multiply and accumulate that they begin to amount to a new system or mindset.

We can cast our minds back over the last few decades and recall the new developments. We can think of Mass in the vernacular, of readers and ministers of the Eucharist, of parish committees, of lay involvement, of collaborative ministry and collaborative leadership.

As we do, perhaps we can conclude that we are now at the stage where parish renewal is more than a series of discrete new initiatives emerging within the inherited system. Perhaps we can say that what we mean by 'parish renewal' is, in the same way as modern science, nothing less than a new mindset.

And not only a new mindset. Just as the worldview of modern science has generated all kinds of technological innovations, so the new mindset of parish renewal has led to new ways of operating, to things being done differently, to new ways of being together as God's people. In the end, parish renewal is not just a new mindset, not just a new theory. It is a new practice, a new way of being Church.

Further Reading

Pope John Paul II. *Christifideles Laici* - Apostolic Exhortation on the Vocation and the Mission of the Lay Faithful in the Church and in the World (1988).

Pope John Paul II. *Redemptoris Missio* - Encyclical Letter on the Permanent Validity of the Church's Missionary Mandate (1990).

Vatican Congregation for the Clergy. *Directory on the Ministry and Life of Priests* (1994).

Bishops' Conference of England and Wales. *The Sign We Give* - Report from the Working Party on Collaborative Ministry (1995).

Dublin Diocesan Committee for Parish Development and Renewal. *Parish Development and Renewal: Presenting the Dublin Experience* (Dublin: Veritas, 1993).

John O'Shea, Declan Lang, Vicky Cosstick, Damian Lundy. *Parish Project: A Resource Book to help Parishes to reflect on their Mission* (London: Harper Collins, 1992).

Peter Coughlan. *The Hour of the Laity: Exploring Christifideles Laici* (Newtown: E. J. Dwyer, 1989).

Enda Lyons. *Partnership in Parish: A Vision for Parish Life, Mission and Ministry* (Dublin: Columba Press, revised edition, 1993).

Allan White. 'Seeking a Theology of the Parish.' *Priests and People,* April 1991, pages 130-133.

Avery Dulles. *Models of the Church* (Dublin: Gill and Macmillan, 1976).

Avery Dulles. 'Imaging the Church for the 1980s.' *Thought* 56 (1981), pages 121-138.

Kenan Osborne. *Priesthood: A History of the Ordained Ministry in the Roman Catholic Church* (New York: Paulist Press, 1988).

Kenan Osborne. *Ministry: Lay Ministry in the Roman Catholic Church* (New York: Paulist Press, 1993).

Daniel Donovan. *What are they Saying about Ministerial Priesthood?* (New York: Paulist Press, 1992).

David Bosch. *Transforming Mission: Paradigm Shifts in the Theology of Mission* (Maryknoll: Orbis Books, 1991).

Loughlan Sofield and Carroll Juliano. *Collaborative Ministry: Skills and Guidelines* (Notre Dame: Ave Maria Press, 1987).

Loughlan Sofield and Donald Kuhn. *The Collaborative Leader: Listening to the Wisdom of God's People* (Notre Dame: Ave Maria Press, 1995).

James Whitehead and Evelyn Whitehead. *The Emerging Laity: Returning Leadership to the Community of Faith* (New York: Doubleday, 1988).

William Bausch. *Ministry: Traditions, Tensions, Transitions* (Mystic, Twenty-Third Publications, 1982).

Paul Bernier. *Ministry in the Church: A Historical and Pastoral Approach* (Mystic, Twenty-Third Publications, 1992).

Thomas O'Meara. *Theology of Ministry* (New York: Paulist Press, 1983).

David Power. *Gifts that Differ: Lay Ministries Established and Unestablished* (New York: Pueblo, 1980).

Mary Cassidy. 'The Bishop's Madness.' *The Furrow,* October 1993, pages 550-553.

Donal Harrington. 'The Church as Home.' *What is Morality?* (Dublin: Columba Press, 1996), pages 214-229.

Catherine Widdicombe. *Group Meetings that Work: A Practical Guide for Working with Different Kinds of Groups* (Slough: St Pauls, 1994).

Anne Hope and Sally Timmel. *Training for Transformation: A Handbook for Community Workers.* (Zimbabwe: Mambo Press, 3 volumes, 1984).

Patricia Prendiville. *Developing Facilitation Skills: A Handbook for Group Facilitators* (Dublin: Combat Poverty Agency, 1995).